T0283892

CHUCO PUNK

American Music Series
Jessica Hopper and Charles L. Hughes, Series Editors

RECENT TITLES IN THE SERIES

Alex Pappademas and Joan LeMay, *Quantum Criminals: Ramblers, Wild Gamblers, and Other Sole Survivors from the Songs of Steely Dan*

Bruce Adams, *You're with Stupid: Kranky, Chicago, and the Reinvention of Indie Music*

Margo Price, *Maybe We'll Make It: A Memoir*

Francesca Royster, *Black Country Music: Listening for Revolutions*

Lynn Melnick, *I've Had to Think Up a Way to Survive: On Trauma, Persistence, and Dolly Parton*

Lance Scott Walker, *DJ Screw: A Life in Slow Revolution*

Eddie Huffman, *John Prine: In Spite of Himself*

David Cantwell, *The Running Kind: Listening to Merle Haggard*

Stephen Deusner, *Where the Devil Don't Stay: Traveling the South with the Drive-By Truckers*

Eric Harvey, *Who Got the Camera? A History of Rap and Reality*

Kristin Hersh, *Seeing Sideways: A Memoir of Music and Motherhood*

Hannah Ewens, *Fangirls: Scenes from Modern Music Culture*

Sasha Geffen, *Glitter Up the Dark: How Pop Music Broke the Binary*

Hanif Abdurraqib, *Go Ahead in the Rain: Notes to A Tribe Called Quest*

Peter Blackstock and David Menconi, Founding Editors

CHUCO PUNK

Sonic Insurgency in El Paso

Tara López

University of Texas Press ⬦ Austin

Copyright © 2024 by Tara López
All rights reserved
Printed in the United States of America
First edition, 2024

Requests for permission to reproduce material from this work should be sent to permissions@utpress.utexas.edu.

♾ The paper used in this book meets the minimum requirements of ANSI/NISO Z39.48-1992 (R1997) (Permanence of Paper).

Library of Congress Cataloging-in-Publication Data

Names: Martin López, Tara, author.
Title: Chuco punk : sonic insurgency in El Paso / Tara Martin López.
Other titles: American music series (Austin, Tex.)
Description: First edition. | Austin : University of Texas Press, 2024. | Series: American music series | Includes index.
Identifiers: LCCN 2023045680
    ISBN 978-1-4773-2967-2 (hardcover)
    ISBN 978-1-4773-2481-3 (paperback)
    ISBN 978-1-4773-2957-3 (pdf)
    ISBN 978-1-4773-2958-0 (epub)
Subjects: LCSH: Punk rock music—Texas—El Paso—History and criticism. | Punk rock music—Social aspects—Texas—El Paso—History. | Punk rock music—Political aspects—Texas—El Paso—History. | Punk rock musicians—Texas—El Paso. | Mexican American musicians—Texas—El Paso. | El Paso (Tex.) —Social life and customs. | BISAC: MUSIC / Genres & Styles / Punk
Classification: LCC ML3534.3 .M374 2024 | DDC 781.6609764/96—dc23/eng/20231017
LC record available at https://lccn.loc.gov/2023045680

doi:10.7560/324813

To all the Chuco punx

CONTENTS

Aligning My Coordinates

EL PASO APPEARS TO BE an unlikely place for a punk rock revolution, but for a little girl growing up in Southern New Mexico, everything special and unique has always been associated with this city in West Texas.

At Val Verde Mobile Home Park, in the small town of Doña Ana, if the sole swing set in the middle of the park was not mobbed with the big kids, I would run out there and wiggle onto a swing. My hope was to propel myself high enough with my short, chubby legs to see beyond the trailer park. Although it was an impossible dream, especially for a four-year-old, I thought I might get a glimpse of the surrounding desert, a "skyrise" in nearby Las Cruces, or even the El Paso my father was always talking about.

My effort was fruitless, but El Paso would continually appear throughout my life. Although my father's family is from the Northern New Mexican town of Taos, he has always spoken with much more kindness and affection for Southern New Mexico, always including El Paso as if it were still part of New Mexico. He is oblivious to neither geography nor history, but according to him, "El Paso just fits in culturally and needs to come back to New Mexico." This sentiment is shared by many other Nuevomexicanos like him. It's as if a bitter romance is embedded in our collective memory, along with a resentment of Texas' claim of New Mexico's largest settlement in the mid-nineteenth century.

A strong affection for El Paso has therefore been omnipresent in my life—an emotional proximity to this city that continues to endure. Punk rock has been an equally intimate and powerful force.

Punk rock is a blitzkrieg of sound that shattered musical conventions. Although the first band described as "punk" in 1966 was the Chicanx band Question Mark and the Mysterians, the birth of punk is often ascribed to the UK in the late 1970s. Bands like X-Ray Spex, the Raincoats, the Slits, the Sex Pistols, and the Clash were the British outposts in this revolution. Across the Atlantic, the Bags, the Zeros, the Plugz, and the Ramones, among many others, held their own in the States. With intensity, irreverence, a do-it-yourself (DIY) ethos, and disdain for the excesses of '70s progressive rock, punk was a stripped-down sonic weapon for everyone, especially the marginalized and disaffected. Despite claims of punk's demise, it has continued to thrive in a variety of permutations, from the early '80s hardcore of Bad Brains and Black Flag to the similarly political but more melodic Fugazi in the early 1990s. The fusion of queer pride, feminism, and punk soon manifested in the queercore of Pansy Division and the Riot Grrrl of Bratmobile and Huggy Bear and Latinx Hardcore of Los Crudos. The heart of punk rock continues to beat strong with the rise of Afro-punk artists like Santigold and Ho99o9, the surfpunk of Tacocat, and the pop-punk of All Thicc in the late twentieth and early twenty-first centuries. Sociologist Nick Crossley vigorously sums it up: "Punk made music matter. . . . Punk was a catalyst, battering a hole in the walls of the popular music world, creating opportunities and encouraging widespread participation."[1]

Punk rock mattered to me and my sister, too.

Once my family left Doña Ana for the big city, my older sister started taking me along to heavy metal and punk shows. One night would be Albuquerque's gigantic Tingley Coliseum with Anthrax, and the next would be the claustrophobic Atomic Theater with punk band D.I. It was sound and rebellion that voiced my confusion and anger about being dirty and poor in the War Zone neighborhood of Albuquerque.

What it did *not* tap into, however, was the deep-seated sexism and racism I not only saw on stage, but in my own life.

It dawned on me that there was no space for me, until Riot Grrrl pried open a space for scores of us in the mid-'90s.

On a trip to the Bay Area to see local Albuquerque punk band Word Salad at Berkeley's punk venue 924 Gilman Street, we were smart enough to stick around for the headliners.

Bikini Kill were the headliners. In all honesty, I remember very little of the Bikini Kill set. What I do remember most poignantly was the community of girls in dresses at the show carrying plastic grocery store bags like purses and being really kind to me. I also remember that Tobi Vail and Kathleen Hanna called out to me, me, of all people. I don't mean this literally. What I mean is that the girls in the audience were no longer just side notes to vigorously be erased from the audience and the music.

No. When Hanna called out, "Hey, girlfriend / I got a proposition, and it goes something like this," she and the entire band saw us girls as relevant and worthy of attention, respect, and focus. My mind was blown, and I became dangerously empowered.

I took that energy to the Launchpad, which became the central punk venue to satiate my voracious appetite for sound in Albuquerque. The punk community, which included a few of the punx I interviewed for this book, created a sense of belonging among fellow outsiders, most of whom were punx of color.

Nevertheless, many of the local bands did not reflect what it was like to grow up in Albuquerque. To me, they sounded like the Beach Boys or The Strokes.

They did not sound like home.

The bands that *did* sound like home were the bands from El Paso who had moved to Albuquerque. Bands like the Chinese Love Beads and Better Off Dead looked and sounded Chicano while bringing a fury of rock and punk to Albuquerque that blew people off their feet.

El Paso native and Chinese Love Beads' drummer Mikey Morales was also my designated driver. He drove me home from the Launchpad countless times, reinforcing my faith in the precept that being kind is punk as fuck.

That impression stuck with me, and despite the intervening decades, my love of punk and for fellow punx, especially punx of color, has endured. As I eventually burrowed myself into academics and emerged as an academic myself, punk rock evolved from a personal passion to the focus of my work.

I have always known that El Paso and punk are actually *the most likely* of pairings, and my research has only reinforced this visceral certainty. While punk is known for its daring subversion, so too is El Paso. Indeed, in the nineteenth century, El Paso's reputation as a criminal outpost of sin was so widespread that its nickname soon became "Chuco," a derivative of the Spanish word for "crooked" or "illegal."[2] El Paso was the natural staging site for a punk revolution.

As a four-year-old on a swing set, I never even got high enough to clear the tops of our trailers and glimpse El Paso, but the momentum I started in Doña Ana in the late '70s has been building for decades, fusing historic, personal, and musical currents in my own biography and setting my personal and professional coordinates for Chuco. On the horizon are the Franklin Mountains, and in their shadow is the rich history of a city that has nourished the songs, bands, zines, flyers, and riots that these amazing punx forged out of history, ingenuity, struggle, community, and, most importantly, love.

CHUCO PUNK

Sonic Insurgency in El Paso

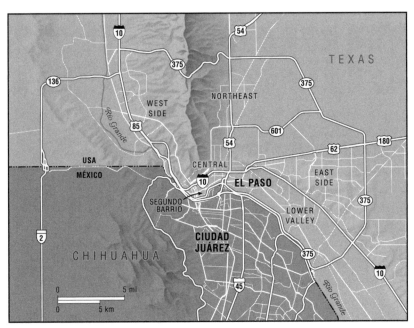

Map of El Paso with regions mentioned in the book

INTRODUCTION

"¡Vamonos pa'l Chuco!"

> Where we come from is between two passes. That's why it's called El Paso.
>
> *Cedric Bixler-Závala, at a live performance of "Invalid Litter Dept.," unknown location and date*

> Chicana/o youth had historically been at the forefront of formulating stylized social statements via the fashion and youth subculture, beginning with the Pachucos and continuing with Chicana Mods in the 1960s.
>
> *Michelle Habell-Pallán,* Loca Motion: The Travels of Chicana and Latina Popular Culture

BEFORE AT THE DRIVE-IN AND The Mars Volta, one of Omar Rodríguez-López's main local bands in El Paso was Jerk. Rodríguez-López's friend Ernesto Ybarra wanted to put his newly minted label Yucky Bus to work, so Ybarra's band, VBF, and Jerk released a split tape in December of 1993 called *To Make Money*.

To celebrate the collaboration, they wanted to have a release party. Sergio "Surge" Mendoza, Ybarra's bandmate, had the perfect house in the Lower Valley region of El Paso to host this massive backyard show. Along with VBF and Jerk, they booked several other local punk bands for this February 1994 show, including Pragmatic, Jim Jone$ and the

Flyer for the VBF/Jerk Tape and Fanzine Release Show, February 1994

KoolAid Kids, Wad, and Debaser. The first fifty punx who paid four bucks to get in got a free copy of the VBF/Jerk cassette tape along with the local *Walk Among the Dead* fanzine. They could also pick up nachos and burritos from Surge's mom, Isabel Valenzuela Mendoza, who was selling them from her kitchen. Soon the cassettes and comic books sold out as the crowd grew from fifty to hundreds of restless punx milling outback, anticipating the onslaught of passionate noise about to explode in the Lower Valley.

Once Lower Valley standouts VBF started playing, two different mosh and skankin' pits developed, revolving like two intense hurricanes against the passive weather map that was Surge's backyard. "You'd see these little dirt clouds coming up from the pits," Surge remembers.

They earned $900 from the show, but according to Surge, after the bands finished playing, two El Paso Police Department helicopters and twenty cop cars descended on the house. Isabel knew that the money from the show would be lost to the cops, so she pushed a panel aside in their roof and hid the earnings there.

Thanks to Surge, Ernesto, Omar, and Isabel's creativity and planning, VBF had enough money to fix their tour van and take their sound on the road. The ferocity and creativity of the Chuco punx was already evident from this one awesome DIY punk show. It's also an ideal entry point into the rich, dynamic, and powerful story of Chuco punk, a unique history that is intimately intertwined with the broader history of cultural resistance in El Paso.

WHY CHUCO PUNK?

While Rodríguez-López's role in this rowdy February '94 punk show highlights the more recognizable musicians from iconic punk band At the Drive-In (ATDI), he and his bandmates were part of a larger web of Chuco punx active at the time. By centering the experiences of the many Chuco punx I interviewed from 2019 to 2023, the critical role this wider punk community played comes into relief. But understanding an entire community can be a daunting undertaking. That's where punk scholars can help connect the dots.

One such scholar is sociologist Nick Crossley. Inspired by Howard Becker's notion of art as a form of collective action, Crossley looks not only at musicians, but also roadies, promoters, and others as participants, which sets a much more expansive and inclusive understanding of these communities centered around music. Really what Crossley recognizes is that community is at the core of punk rock, and it's likewise at the core of the Chuco punk scene.[1] While more notable bands like Sparta, for instance, are integral to understanding this scene, they are just one chord in the broader composition of sound and connection that is necessary to understand punk rock in Chuco.

Women like Isabel who had VBF's back in 1994 were as much a part of this community as the bands on stage. Examining spaces like the houses where these shows were played, the recording studios, the Kinko's where flyers were surreptitiously made, and the kitchens where young punx were fed allows us to uncover the dynamic ways in which women played a central role in Chuco punk's inception and development. These roles provided excitement and opportunity but were also subject to gendered limitations.

Understanding the history of women in Chuco punk is necessary for understanding this scene, and it's important for the punk community to understand and reckon with the ways in which women were often marginalized within our ranks. In the iconic '70s British punk zine *Sniffin' Glue*, editor Mike P. made clear how many male punks felt about women in the scene when he wrote, "Punks are not girls, if it comes to the crunch we'll have no option but to fight back."[2] In many punk histories, for that matter, women continue to be ignored, or they are condemned to appallingly condescending and incomplete footnotes. By focusing on punx that identify as women, British cultural theorist Angela McRobbie unpacked their unique forms of participation in subcultures in her 1991 book, *Feminism and Youth Culture: From Jackie to Just Seventeen*. While writing the book, she did not give up when she could not find masses of girls in subcultures, but instead changed her focus to more domestic, interior settings to follow the rise of girls' youth culture.[3] Scholar Laurine LeBlanc's *Pretty in Punk: Girl's Gender Resistance in a Boy's Subculture* delivers a study of girls in punk which is most resonant to Chuco punk. LeBlanc writes of how punk provided a range of complex experiences for girls, but at its core, it provided them with a vehicle to challenge broader forms of sexism and "retain a strong sense of self" in the face of sexist hostility within the scene.[4]

In her seminal work *Revenge of the She-Punks: A Feminist Music History from Poly Styrene to Pussy Riot*, punk scholar Vivien Goldman sought to throw "a rope bridge" across "the chasm of deliberate cultural erasure" of women in punk.[5] Likewise in this book, the close to twenty punx I interviewed who identify as women will come to the fore, and the contributions of punx of color and queer punx in Chuco will play a significant role throughout. However, since interviewees rarely disclosed whether they were members of the LGBTQ community, there will be more do to on the part of future researchers to spotlight the multiple roles women and queer punx played in the creation of this Chucotown soundtrack.

When VBF and Jerk were taking the stage in the 1990s, "Hispanics"[6] made up 69 percent of El Paso's population,[7] and today, they make up 81.6 percent of the population.[8] Statistics aside, those punx creating that dust storm from their skankin' were mostly Brown, but that fact is not reflected in popular and scholarly representations of punk. In 1986, columnist Mykel Board, for instance, proclaimed in the seminal punk zine *Maximum Rocknroll* that "punk was the first white music since the 1960s psychedelic stuff"[9] and in 2010, pop culture historian Dewar MacLeod declared that "Hardcore was white music."[10] Punx are not alone in making such blunt declarations. Some scholars have portrayed LA punks from 1977 to 1983 as suburban white kids engaged in a self-imposed exile of otherness and insecurity that was authentically experienced by the poor and people of color.[11]

These slapdash assertions and limited arguments reinforce popular images of a sneering (white, British, male) Sid Vicious as the face of punk rock, erasing punx of color from public consciousness and history. These writers made sweeping conclusions based solely on their own personal experiences with punk rock. While white-Black and white-Hispanic segregation has declined in the twenty-first century, most Black Americans continue to live in the most segregated areas of the United States, followed by Latinos. If the United States was and is so segregated, why would punk scenes be any different?[12]

Thankfully, in the last two decades, there have been powerful challenges to such limited views, most notably in scholar Michelle Habell-Pallán's seminal work on 1980s Chicanx/Latinx punk in Los Angeles,

Loca Motion: The Travels of Chicana and Latina Popular Culture. Although taking a broader focus on popular culture, Habell-Pallán also takes on punk rock specifically and argues that "mainstream representations of punk represent punk culture as a monolithic, white-boy-only fad. In fact, punk had various and competing strains; it was not one thing."[13] With a particularly evocative and detailed account of Chicanas like Alicia Armendariz ("Alice Bag" from the Bags) and Teresa Covarrubias (lead singer of the Brat), Habell-Pallán paved the way for future punk researchers to understand the historic role of women of color, especially Chicanas/Latinas, in punk rock history. The history of Chuco punk illustrates how punk is not, and has never been, just white and male. Chuco punk was Brown and down, and so too, is punk rock.[14]

Just like the distorted understandings of punk, images of El Paso as a barren land of tumble weeds or merely "as a dusty bowl on the cusp of the US-Mexican border notorious for its drug traffic, sweltering heat, a population of a million and the mentality of a small town" are rife in popular culture.[15] If it's not the Marty Robbins tributes, it will be the Pace Picante sauce commercials that preserve in amber an image of the city infused with a white cowboy nostalgia, with Mexicans and Indigenous people as exoticized backdrops. Moreover, such primitive, Wild West images of El Paso belie the fact that El Paso has been and remains an industrial giant at the forefront of geopolitical developments throughout the twentieth and twenty-first centuries. Scholars like Michelle Habell-Pallán and Indigenous theorist Philip Deloria Jr. encourage us to strip away such colonial and stereotypical images to understand these communities on their own terms.[16]

When we shuck such colonial lenses, we see El Paso as a city of socio-political significance and a hotbed of cutting-edge popular culture. At the beginning of the twentieth century, the city hosted ASARCO and Phelps Dodge, the largest mining and smelter conglomerates in the nation. El Paso historian Monica Perales points out that the city was a "veritable nexus of a modern railroad and mining empire" rather than the "rough-and-tumble frontier town its local historians are often fond of cultivating in collective memory."[17] The city's significance at the end of the twentieth century and early twenty-first centuries made it also the source of the United States' current immigration enforcement strategy. Indeed, the city is a home base to so many federal law enforcement agencies that El Paso is consistently ranked as one of the safest cities in the United States.[18]

In addition to being a leader of economic and political transformation, it has been the cradle of transformative cultural innovation. Most notably, El Paso/Juárez's was the cradle of the slang, style, and sound of *pachuquismo*, the historic counterculture of the zoot suit. According to historians like Gerardo Licón, the recorded site of the first pachuco use of caló slang appeared on the corner of 8th and Florence in El Paso's Segundo Barrio in the early 1930s.[19] The ties between *pachuquismo* and punk rock are neither tenuous nor arbitrary. According to East LA musician Mark Guerrero, "The Mexican American pachucos who originated in the 1930s were the original punks."[20] The Chuco punk revolution in the '90s and 2000s was not an isolated outburst but was part of a broader and historic conflagration of cultural resistance characteristic of an economically, politically, and culturally vibrant city.

Pachucas, El Paso rock 'n' rollers like Long John Hunter and Bobby Fuller, and punx were not just passive recipients of this historic legacy of the city and region; they were active in reconfiguring it. Instead of taking for granted that places simply exist statically in space, historian Monica Perales in her research on El Paso's Smeltertown argues that people are active in re-creating space to create meaning and community. Punx in El Paso did the same. In this case, punx had music as their focus, but geographer Ray Hudson adds that music "plays a very particular and sensuous role in place making."[21]

This transformative element of Chuco punk is especially significant considering the history of marginalization and segregation that provided the context of the 1970s to the early 2000s. "Lower Valley," "Northeast," "Central," and "West Side" were geographic designations for punx and suggested broader class and racial/ethnic divisions within the city. Indeed, the transformation of garages, backyards, bedrooms, ditches, and Kinko's copy centers into sites of movement, creativity, and sound also illustrate how these punx made El Paso and its space malleable.

Even more compelling is that Chuco Punx transgressed the international border between El Paso and Juárez and forged a unified Juárez/El Paso reflective of Chicana feminist scholar and cultural/queer theorist Gloria Anzaldúa's fluid understandings of a borderland as "a vague and undetermined place created by the emotional residue of an unnatural boundary," instead of a border that is fixed and divisive.[22] Scholar María Josefina Saldaña-Portillo connects such fluidity to Indigenous understandings of border communities like Juárez/El Paso, which are not divided, but rather consist of "one cultural landscape."[23]

Chuco punx defied the borders and limits of a sterile, pacified, mapped El Paso, and rearranged it into a larger, dynamic, creative, fluid, and a *more, but not completely*, egalitarian site embodied by its nickname. The unified cultural landscape that the El Paso punx created was that of Chuco.

CHUCO-COORDINATES

This book covers the history and sound of El Paso from the late nineteenth century to the early twenty-first century and examines the utility of Chuco culture as a battleground and wellspring of sonic resistance. This history is rich and exciting, but so much is missing. Indeed, not every story could be told. Nevertheless, as songwriter Isaac Brock observes, nothing in writing is complete. "More often than not, you got to quit trying to get there, and whatever's there, you hope the next thing you do answers that question."[24]

What's left is the soundtrack . . .

THE SOUNDTRACK

In the introduction to the podcast *Louder Than a Riot*, Rodney Carmichael explains, "If a riot 'is the language of the unheard' like Dr. King once said, then rap is the definitive soundtrack."[25] Chuco punk was also an expression of ignored voices that refused to be silenced, but these outbursts always had a context. Right before playing the song "Invalid Litter Dept." live, At the Drive-In lead singer Cedric Bixler-Závala made sure to root the song in its location, both geographic and emotional: "Where we come from is between two passes. That's why it's called El Paso." He knew that it was crucial to establish the backdrop because so much conflict, convergence, and creativity marks El Paso's history, culture, and society. The confluence nourished the murmurs, shouts, and songs of the people of this city and region. In the process, they forged a new, alternative, and sometimes subversive language and identity: Chuco.

In backyard shows, in bedrooms refashioned into recording studios, on cassette tapes and in zines, they were making their own noise, charting their own maps, and inventing their own language. They were arranging their own soundtrack, a Chucotown soundtrack.

Press play now.

"PACHUCO BOOGIE"

Culture, Music, and History of Chuco

Raúl Díaz: ¿Ese, dónde está la lleva pues?
Don Tosti: Nel, ese, pues si no voy ese.
Vengo del paciente ves. Un lugar que
Que le dicen El Paso, nomas que de allá vienen
los pachucos como yo eh.

*Cuarteto Don Ramón Sr. (Edmundo Martínez Tostado, aka
Don Tosti), "Pachuco Boogie," 1948*

EDMUNDO MARTÍNEZ TOSTADO WAS A rebel from the start.

Born in El Paso's Segundo Barrio in 1923 to a mother from El Paso and a father from Santa Fe, New Mexico, he started getting in trouble at an early age. When he was seven years old, his family decided to rein him in by making him take two-hour music lessons every day of the week. According to Tostado, he had to comply, "or they would beat the pie out of me."[1] Nevertheless, the truculent Tostado was soon recognized as a musical prodigy, and two years later he was playing second violin for the El Paso Symphony Orchestra.[2]

His rebellion and sound did not stop there.

When he moved to Los Angeles in 1939, he found that people didn't like the name Martínez Tostado, so he soon became "Tosti" and, then, "Don Tosti." Although his name became white-washed, Tostado used the moniker, his musical ability, and his cultural pride to create a sound that was formative to the rise of *pachuquismo*. Taking a more subversive approach to music, Tostado embraced the scat and jazz style of African Americans, blended with the caló slang of pachucos in his 1948 song "Pachuco Boogie." It was an immediate hit and became the first Mexican American recording to sell one million copies.[3] Despite its widespread popularity, it had particular resonance as "an anthem among Mexican American youth during the late 1940s as it showcased the pachuco caló and glorified zoot style."[4] Most importantly, Don Tosti specifically calls out his hometown as the cradle of *pachuquismo* in the song when Raúl Díaz asks where Tosti is going:

No man, I'm not going but coming
From El Paciente, you see
A place called El Paso
That's where the pachucos like me come from, eh.[5]

It is telling that both the name of *pachuquismo* and its central songwriter were from El Paso—from Chuco—revealing the layers of cultural resistance that predated Chuco punx, and even Don Tosti. More than just a list of significant historical and musical markers, El Paso was a site of cutting-edge thought, politics, and culture. As far back as the seventeenth century, Spanish colonizers and later Anglo Americans made concerted efforts to suppress resistance among communities of color in this region. These communities, especially the Mexican community, were both culturally and politically disobedient, which gave voice to changes sonically, stylistically, and legally, with national and international repercussions.

Mexican cultural resistance defied political, geographic, and cultural boundaries, thereby redefining El Paso into the more rebellious and culturally rich Chuco, a site of cultural resistance that would feed into the reservoir of punk ingenuity by the end of the 1970s.

This story of Don Tosti guides us to a deeper history of sonic, spatial, social, and political resistance, and sets the stage for the punk revolution on the horizon.

THROWING DOWN IN THE ARENA OF CULTURE

In the late 1890s, Owen P. White decried how El Paso supposedly once was "a town of twelve thousand that was 80 percent adobe and 92 percent sinners" but by then had become "75 percent brick and only 90 percent sinners."[6] From the 1890s to the 1930s, El Paso's reputation as "sin city" was interlaced here with the potent and contrasting symbols of adobe versus brick representing the cultural conflict that permeated the area for decades. Not only were Anglo Americans trying to exert control over Indigenous and Mexican communities in the area, but with the Southern Pacific Railroad's arrival in 1881, they tried to control Chinese and Black communities, too. This city, rich with a multicultural milieu, also stoked disgust, especially around interracial relationships. US Boundary Commissioner John Russell Bartlett, who was responsible for surveys along the Mexico/US border, described residents of the city as "masses . . . [of] a mixed breed possessing none of the virtues of their European ancestors, but all their vices, with those of the aborigines superadded."[7] Bartlett's particular emphasis on the racial mixing that supposedly characterized the city illustrates the boundary crossing present at El Paso's inception. What Owens and Bartlett have in common is their concern over indomitable communities of color and their influence throughout the city.

The two did have cause for concern. For centuries, Indigenous, Mexican, Black, and Chinese communities in the city had engaged in cultural, political, and spatial insurgency.

Spanish colonizers were the first to see such "aboriginal vices" as deeply threatening, and they made every effort to exert cultural control and domination over the vibrant Indigenous communities in what became known as "El Paso del Norte." When the Spanish colonized the area, naming it "The Mission of Our Lady of Guadalupe" in 1659, it was already an Indigenous interstate highway of economic and cultural significance. In particular, the Sumas and Mansos were already rooted in the El Paso Valley, but Spanish brutality and cultural persecution would soon force other Indigenous peoples into the region. Spanish colonizers forced the Tiguas and Piros into slavery in New Mexico and outlawed their religious dances, along with their ceremonial masks and prayer sticks, which they destroyed. The Spanish flogged, imprisoned, and sometimes hanged Indigenous keepers of this religious and cultural knowledge.[8] Soon after the successful Pueblo Revolt of 1680 in New Mexico, the Spanish forced the Tiguas and Piros south, where they founded the communities of Ysleta del Sur, Senacú, and Socorro. The efforts of colonizers to suppress music and dance is woven into the history of the area.

Efforts to erase Indigenous communities gained further momentum in the late nineteenth century. Hundreds of Tigua and Piro descendants lived in areas like Ysleta and Socorro, but Anglo-Americans classified them as "mixed-blooded Mexicans" instead of "mixed-blooded Indians."[9] The theft of Indigenous lands in El Paso did not stop in the seventeenth century. In 1858, for instance, El Paso judge Josiah Crosby created the fraudulent Ascarate Land Grant. The fabrication of this land grant compounded by his connections in the Texas state legislature facilitated his dispossession of Piro lands that make up the valuable sites of Ascarate Park, the El Paso Airport, and part of Fort Bliss today.[10] The traditions and communities continued to endure. Indeed, Ysleta del Sur Pueblo later became the only pueblo and one of only three federally recognized tribes in the state of Texas.[11]

The growth of the railroads in the region also contributed to this rich culture. Mexico recruited Chinese laborers, for instance, to build the Mexican Central Railroad. Such employment, along with Chinese Exclusion Acts in the United States, made Juárez/El Paso a significant corridor for the Chinese to enter the US and, sometimes, settle in the region. In this era from the 1880s to the 1920s, the Chinese population in El Paso increased from the low hundreds to 1,000.[12] Those Chinese railroad laborers eventually founded laundries and restaurants that were located in South El Paso.[13] Rather than acquiesce to the confines of their ghettoization and broader racist oppression in the face of a nascent Border Patrol, the Chinese community eventually constructed a vast honeycomb of subterranean tunnels under Chinatown to avoid the harassment of immigration officials and the hostility of their fellow El Pasoans in the early twentieth century.[14]

For the Black community, El Paso was both an artery to freedom and a final destination. El Paso was a key entryway to Mexico with up to four thousand slaves fleeing the United States for Mexico in 1855.[15] Immediately after the Civil War, Black regiments were stationed at Fort Bliss, and by 1877, Black soldiers had firmly rooted themselves in the city.[16] The attraction to El Paso was, in part, due to the established Black community, but also to the freedom Black El Pasoans experienced relative to the rest of the South. For instance, El Pasoan David Kirk's grandfather migrated from the Dallas/Waco area to El Paso in the early twentieth century because, according to Kirk, his grandfather saw that in El Paso, "the Black and Brown communities have the opportunity to flourish." The key sites of Black settlement were in Segundo Barrio and, for Black and Mexican railroad workers after 1881, in the Lincoln Park neighborhood on the East Side of El Paso. It was not until the 1970s that Black and Mexican residents of Lincoln Park were permitted to cross Yandell St. since that street formed the southern border of an all-white neighborhood.[17]

The rapidly increasing Mexican population became the focal point of some of the most vicious forms of oppression. Due to the outbreak of the Mexican Revolution, from 1900 to 1916, the Mexican born population in El Paso increased from 5,151 to 32,724.[18] The Immigration Law of 1917, then, began to restrict movements between Mexico and the United States, and part of such restrictions involved delousing Mexicans passing into the US because Mexicans were feared to be carrying typhus into the country. That year, 127,173 Mexicans were deloused with Zyklon B and bathed in gasoline at the Santa Fe International Bridge. To further exacerbate the humiliation, customs officials took private photos of the Mexican women forced to strip naked in this process. Nevertheless, women were not passive in this degradation, and on January 28, 1917, a seventeen-year-old maid from Juárez, Carmelita Torres, declined to bathe in gasoline and convinced thirty other women around her to also refuse. Such rebellion was much more contagious than the supposed typhus threat, and soon two hundred Mexican women joined Torres and blocked traffic on the Santa Fe International Bridge. The emboldened women's actions then came to fever pitch. According to an *El Paso Times* article from the time, as the cavalry arrived to quell the insurgency, the undeterred women began to "claw and tear at the tops of passing cars. The glass rear windows of the autos were torn out, the tops torn to pieces and parts of fittings such as lamps and horns were torn away." The women's collective power rendered the cavalry powerless, and they effectively shut down and seized the border crossing for two days straight. Although the riot forced Mexican officials to issue certificates for people to cross that their counterparts in El Paso begrudgingly accepted, the fumigations continued for the next forty years.[19] Nevertheless, Torres was one of many people who set the insurgent tone and rhythm of Chuco. The rebellion that became known as the "El Paso Bath Riots of 1917" was an early effort by women in El Paso to preserve their bodily integrity, part of a larger grassroots movement to transform the seemingly unyielding international border into something more pliant, reaffirming a broader geography of Chuco.

The insurgency of women like Torres and the rise of these new and robust communities coincided with the rise of policies which sought to limit the power and influence of people of color in El Paso. In 1901, more than a decade before the El Paso-Juárez Bath Riots, the City Council passed a powerful vagrancy ordinance. Aimed primarily at Mexicans and enforced by El Paso's first Hispanic policeman, Roman S. González, the ordinance prohibited people, primarily Mexicans, from congregating on city streets and sidewalks.[20] El Paso was not the only municipality with policies that restricted the space of Mexicans and Mexican Americans. Similar "anti-vagrancy" laws were passed in Los Angeles, part of the broader California state Vagrancy Act of 1855, commonly known as the "Greaser Act," which aimed to crack down on any "idle Mexican," meaning those of "Spanish [or] Indian blood" and especially those who "go armed and are not peaceable and quiet persons."[21] Such attacks on the freedom of Mexicans to claim space reveal how space was a focal point to subjugate Indigenous and Mexican peoples and their cultures.

Racist violence accompanied these racist laws. When Pancho

Villa's soldiers killed eighteen American Smelting and Refining Company (ASARCO) engineers in Mexico in 1916, the subsequent funeral in El Paso sparked a riot. More specifically, groups of Anglos met to discuss lynching "Mexican leaders" in El Paso. Street altercations between Mexicans and Anglos ensued and accelerated into a mob of 1,500 Anglo men, soldiers, and boys storming through El Paso attacking Mexicans. Mexicans mobilized with clubs and other weapons to fend off Anglo attacks. General Pershing and army troops were called in to quell the riot, but the racial oppression continued at the ballot box five years later.[22]

By the early 1920s, the Ku Klux Klan had stoked fears of not merely the threat of Mexicans, but the influence of Mexican culture itself, as a galvanizing political issue. Frontier Klavern No. 100 was established in El Paso in 1921, and its commitment to 'strive for the maintenance of white supremacy' found a rapt audience among many in the city who "wanted to curb Mexican influence in local affairs and firmly assert Anglo dominance."[23] Moreover, the Klan's social morality that focused on dress, speech, and sexual behavior resonated with many Anglo residents at this time. For instance, in the 1920s, Anglo youth regularly crossed into Juárez to drink alcohol and enjoy jazz music. One customs inspector's outrage underlined the anxiety building up in the city when he declared, "I would rather see my daughter in her coffin than to see her go over that bridge to Juárez and begin taking 'just a drink or two.' That's the way they go to hell."[24]

The Klan saw such geographic and unrepentant moral transgressions as threats, and school reform became their first line of defense against such perceived moral degradation. The undercurrent of intense racialization of Mexicans further intensified the Klan's political aspirations. After the Treaty of Guadalupe Hidalgo of 1848 provided citizenship to the over 100,000 Mexicans living in the former Mexican territories, these newly minted Mexican Americans were categorized racially as white. However, by the early twentieth century, right when the Klan in El Paso was in its ascendancy, Mexicans were racialized as non-white. In 1921, when all aliens were forbidden from voting, Mexicans in El Paso who were in the process of naturalization were barred from the franchise.[25] Subsequently, in 1922, several Klan candidates took key seats on the El Paso School Board. The school board advocated for more school funding, but also renamed schools for "Texas heroes" such as James Bowie and Stephen F. Austin. They went one step too far, however, when they changed El Paso High School's name to "Sam Houston High." The name change triggered such outrage the high school reassumed its name.[26] Indeed, the early twentieth century highlights white supremacist efforts to obliterate any vestige of Mexican culture, history, and power from El Paso's landscape.

The Klan's brief era of political influence reinforced long-standing elements of segregation already present within the school system. Their justification was a potent and pernicious form of eugenics as Mexican students were segregated from Anglo students because, according to historian Monica Perales, they were seen as "mentally incapable of succeeding in American classrooms."[27] Black students attended the segregated Douglass Colored School on the South Side of El Paso.[28] It was not until the beginning of the twentieth century when the Aoy School was opened that Mexican students in El Paso were finally afforded a non-trades focused education.[29]

The subversive sounds of corridos would be one of the bold soundtracks to confront this oppressive environment. Corridos were the punk rock of the era, with these ballads being made by and for ordinary people primarily from 1836 to the late 1930s. Chicana theorist Gloria Anzaldúa emphasizes the importance of corridos for Chicanos because they were "about Mexican heroes who do valiant deeds against Anglo oppressors. . . . These folk musicians and folk songs are our chief cultural mythmakers, and they made our hard lives bearable."[30] The popular, reaffirming, and informative nature of corridos, especially during the Mexican Revolution, inspired some of the most noted Chicano scholars to engage in detailed research on the genre. One of the most notable is Américo Paredes, who recognized how corridos were, indeed, a sonic tool among Mexicans and Mexican Americans to resist Anglo Texan domination.[31]

One way they resisted Anglo domination was to spotlight the lives of thieves and criminals as folk heroes. "El Contrabando del Paso," was one of the most famous corridos made and seen as "a precursor to the popular narcocorridos of today." The song was written and recorded during Prohibition (1920–1933). Gabriel Jara Franco, the likely composer, details how "smuggling is very nice," and profitable, but most of the song follows him on the train from El Paso to Leavenworth prison in Kansas after being caught.[32] Although the corrido speaks to the freedom of smuggling, it also serves as a warning:

> Smuggling is very nice, you can make a lot of money,
> but friends, do not forget what a prisoner must suffer. (. . .)
> This is the ballad of the contraband of El Paso.[33]

Another way they resisted Anglo control was to highlight the lives and adventures of Mexican women. Feminist scholar María Herrera-Sobek argues that corridos are not a male genre but a male-dominated one. A reflection of this male-dominance in corridos are themes that stress women's need to conform to gender norms. Nevertheless, Herrera-Sobek believes the stress on making women behave that appears in corridos can also shed light on Mexican women's freedom, too. For her, "The very need to structure such corridos indicates that Mexican women were not as submissive and passive as we have been led to believe. If they had been [submissive and passive], there would be no need for such songs."[34]

Aside from advising women to be pious and avoid foolishness, corridos also document the efforts of *soldaderas* fighting during the Mexican Revolution. Immortalized in photos of women courageously bearing rifles, wearing bandoleras and long skirts, corridos were instrumental ways of documenting their bravery. Scholar Elizabeth Salas emphasizes the crucial role warrior women played in Mesoamerican and Mexican history, and in corridos like "El Corrido the Juana Gallo:"

Entre ruidos de cañones y metrallas	Among the noise of cannons and shrapnel
surgió una historia popular	comes forth a popular story
de una joven que apodaban Juana Gallo	about a youth called Juana Gallo
por ser valiente a no dudar.	because she was valiant without a doubt.
Siempre al frente de las tropas se encontraba	Always at the front of the troops you saw her
peleando como cualquier Juan	fighting like all other soldiers
en campaña ni un pelón se escapaba	in battle no federal solider escaped her
sin piedad se los tronaba su enorme pistolón	without mercy she shot them with her big pistol.[35]

The subversive identity brandished as a medal of cultural resistance present in corridos soon found expression in El Paso's homegrown *pachuquismo*. The pressures from the Anglo riots of 1916, compounded by municipal policies that forced Mexican men off the streets and into segregated schools, fueled a conflagration of stylistic and sonic insurrection. *Pachuquismo* is commonly associated with zoot suitors from Los Angeles and characterized by its oppositional and distinctive style. Nevertheless, scholars agree that *pachuquismo* originated somewhere between El Paso's Segundo Barrio and Juárez between 1910 and 1939.[36]

Although largely associated with Mexican youth, the culture of the zoot suit was also developed and embraced among Black, white, Asian, and Indigenous youth throughout the United States. Within *pachuquismo*, fashion was also central to this identity. Pachucas, oftentimes referred to as "chukas," "zooter girls," "cholitas," "slick chicks," or "malinches," donned distinctive styles. El Pasoan Delia Chávez, who eventually moved to East Los Angeles, recounts how she donned a gabardine zoot suit, composed of a "finger-tip" coat and full skirt accompanied by a dark bouffant beautifully piled on her head. Other components of pachuca style included heavy mascara and lipstick, tattoos, fitted skirts, and bobby socks.[37] For men, the zoot suit consisted of a double-breasted suit with wide shoulders that reached their knees. These were combined with baggy pants, or *tramos*, and a long pocket chain at the side.[38]

This style was more than significant to pachucas and pachucos; it was seen as a threat to white hegemony. In June of 1943, white military personnel and civilians in Los Angeles physically attacked primarily *pachucos*, stripped them of their zoot suits in front of onlookers, and arrested them for vagrancy and disturbing the peace. In what became known as the Zoot Suit Riots, the weeklong series of assaults highlighted how menacing *pachuquismo* was to white supremacy.[39] Don Tosti and his fellow musicians in Cuarteto Don Ramón Sr. released "Pachuco Boogie" five years later. In the song, pride in his zoot suit comes to the fore as he parades it around LA.

Me vine acá al Los Ca ve	I came to L.A., see,
Me vine a parar gara	I came to show off my clothes[40]

Tosti's unabashed pride in his rebellious style was echoed among pachucos back home in El Paso. Chuco punk Alex Martínez interviewed one El Paso pachuco in the early twenty-first century, and the interviewee was adamant that people know:

> Many Mexicanos misinterpreted that culture. Pachucos were seen as aggressive, but they had to be. The main motive of a Pachuco was to call attention to oneself. What does dressing like that have to do with identity? It says: "Nosotros vamos hacer lo que queremos hacer!"[41]

Rather than something merely superficial, *pachuquismo's* style was an expression of ethnic pride set against the overt racism of the day.

The spread of *pachuquismo* illustrates the way it resonated with other youths of the early to mid-twentieth century. Chuco has been at the vanguard of popular cultural for decades.

Despite *pachuquismo*'s El Paso roots, Arizona native Marty Robbins' 1959 "El Paso" has become the most recognizable (though problematic) ballad associated with the city. Indeed, the song views the city through a variety of stereotypical tropes, such as the cowboy meeting the "Mexican temptress" and the intro infused with "Spanish-flavored" guitars.[42] El Paso was already an industrial trade giant by the mid-1950s, so at heart, this was an outsider's nostalgic gaze, superimposing characterizations of the long-lost Wild West on the city. He continued with the same theme with the 1955 "Feelina (From El Paso)" and the 1976 "El Paso City." The cartoonish and stereotypical nature of the characters in these songs cannot be overstated. Not only do they reflect the popular stereotypes of the city noted earlier, but they have even tainted Texas political culture. For instance, in the early 1980s, El Paso State Representative Paul Moreno decried the city's lack of political heft in the state legislature: "[My fellow legislators] still think we're [El Paso] Rosa's Cantina—a little border village."[43] This was an outsider's view, imbued with colonial boasting and demeaning characterizations. The song revealed the need for communities in El Paso, especially Mexican communities, to tell their own stories, and make their own noise.

By the time Robbins had released this quaint and seriously limited tune, El Paso had undergone dramatic changes. Prior to World War II, the federal government created two hundred maps of major metropolitan areas, El Paso being one of them. These maps, eventually known as redlining maps, reaffirmed the segregation that had gained steam in the early twentieth century. Areas such as Kern place, which were predominantly white, were rated worthy of federally subsidized home loans, and predominantly Black and Brown neighborhoods like Segundo Barrio and Lincoln Park were redlined and deemed "hazardous." Moreover, the construction of I-10 and Highways 54 and 110 went directly through the Black Lincoln Park community, leaving only the remnants of this once thriving Black community in its place.[44]

The twentieth century also signaled transformative points of change, especially politically. In 1924, El Paso physician Dr. Lawrence

Nixon, for instance, brought his challenge to an all-white Democratic primary when he was barred from receiving a ballot in the Democratic primary. With the support of the NAACP, Dr. Nixon fought a twenty-year battle, which was eventually successful. In 1927 the Supreme Court, in *Nixon v. Herndon*, ruled that Dr. Nixon had been unlawfully denied his right to vote, laying the basis for subsequent achievements in the realm of voting rights.[45] Soon after Nixon's victory in 1944, "colored sections" were also removed from El Paso streetcars and buses, and it became the first school system in Texas to desegregate.[46]

The most significant change was the election of Raymond Telles, with family roots in Ysleta, as El Paso's first Mexican American mayor in 1957. His election, while the apparent harbinger of racial progress in the city, was met with dismay by some. When Telles won, a local businessman declared: 'How can we hold our heads up in the state of Texas when we have a Mexican mayor?'[47] This response should not be surprising, however, considering that a mere three years before, the federal government had deported 35,000 undocumented El Pasoans as part of "Operation Wetback."[48] Moreover, political representation among Mexican Americans in both El Paso and the entire state of Texas continued to be paltry, at best. From 1881 to 1951, no Mexican Americans were elected to El Paso's City Council.[49] Statewide, representation wasn't any better years later. In 1960, there were only three "Hispanic" state representatives of the 150 in the legislature. That's just 2 percent, and only one "Hispanic" served in the Texas State Senate that same year.[50]

By the end of the 1950s, faced with the pressure to conform to political oppression and attempts at cultural erasure, communities of color began engaging in sustained cultural and political resistance. From Carmelita Torres to Dr. Lawrence Nixon, communities throughout the city took space in their own hands to reshape it in a more just and dynamic Chuco. And the soundtrack took the form of pugnacious corridos documenting the lives of pachucas and pachucos boogying their way down forbidden streets with a sound and style to unsettle the power structure.

The sounds would soon change . . . with rock 'n' roll and punk striking dissonant chords in discordant times.

ROCKIN' IN CHUCO: 1950S AND '60S

Despite the oppressive headwinds in the face of incremental racial progress, by the 1950s, Chuco had become the site of a rock 'n' roll renaissance. One of the first to spark this musical creativity was Black musician John Thurman Hunter Jr., who had moved to El Paso in 1957, the year Telles was elected to office. Originally from Louisiana, he eventually made it to Texas. From 1957 to 1970 he played in Juárez's Lobby Bar as "Long John Hunter." Although not as segregated as the rest of Texas, few white or Mexican bars in El Paso granted entrance to Black customers. The Lobby Bar was located along Juárez's main artery and was accompanied by bars catering to Black Americans and Black Mexicans from Juárez; clubs like the Ebony Club, El Nuevo Harlem, El Gato Negro, and Club Ritmo in the Black neighborhood of Juárez called La Mariscal.[51]

Hunter was relentless, playing seven nights a week at the Lobby Bar for thirteen years. He was known to describe those nights as, "a party from eight o' clock 'til 'please, go home' in the morning."[52] Hunter's biggest hit, "El Paso Rock," released in 1961, is an upbeat homage to the city. The only lyrics are "El Paso Rock," and the intermittent encouragement of "Keep on' going, you hear!" "Keep going, again!" as Hunter and the listener just keep boppin' along.

At a slower pace, Hunter takes the listener on a cruise in his Cadillac through El Paso in "Border Town Blues."

> Down in Ol' El Paso
> Where the girls are really fine.
> Come down to Ol' El Paso
> And I'll get you one of these girls like mine.[53]

Hunter's unstoppable energy onstage and firm connection to El Paso brought the likes of Buddy Holly, James Brown, Etta James, and the young Bobby Fuller to the Lobby Bar.[54] Like Hunter, Fuller was not born in El Paso, but the area soon permeated his music. The rockabilly sounds of Buddy Holly, who had been recording in nearby Clovis, New

Mexico, were especially influential on Fuller's meteoric rise. Fuller was so focused on music that he built a homemade engineering booth in his house on the East Side of El Paso on Album Avenue, and it was there where he recorded "You're in Love" with local band the Embers in 1961.

Like Hunter, Fuller was relentlessly ambitious in his search for sound. When, in 1962, he formed the Bobby Fuller Four with Dalton Powell on drums and his brother Randy on bass, the stage was set for his brief but significant career. As Fuller began to gain more and more notoriety, El Paso sought to make an explicit shift to claim him as a hometown hero. In September 1964, the *El Paso Times* proclaimed, "England has the Beatles, but El Paso has Bobby."[55]

Local radio and TV legend Steve Crosno described Fuller's onstage magnetism: "He had an incredible presence. Once he came on, you couldn't take your eyes off him."[56] Fuller's unique charisma was powerful, and the Bobby Fuller Four's rendition of the Sonny Curtis song "I Fought the Law" in 1964 brought them attention from Del-Fi, a label in Hollywood. The Fullers then moved to Los Angeles, and their iconic song became a Billboard hit in March 1966. Just four months later, in July of 1966, Fuller was found dead in his car, supposedly of suicide.

Although Fuller's life had ended abruptly, Crosno's influence continued to infuse the El Paso Valley with melody and soul. In 1961, Crosno was the first El Paso disc jockey to play Spanish-language music on English-speaking stations, and it was this effort to bridge cultural divides that was his most distinctive and legendary characteristic. For eight years he was the host of the weekly *Crosno Hop*, on El Paso television. Crosno's influence became so ingrained in the city that in 1967, the mayor of El Paso named June 9 Steve Crosno Day.[57] Crosno also started the Frogdeath label that carried surf and soul bands, and he had a studio in his home which he offered to the local band the Night-Dreamers so they could record their hit "Mr. Pitiful."[58] He obviously built an enduring legacy. In the '90s, "I Love Crosno" was often printed on flyers for punk shows, and "I Love Crosno" stickers continue to appear all over El Paso to this day.

El Paso's rock 'n' roll heyday of the '50s and '60s underlines the city's sonic radiance. Long John Hunter's unstoppable sound, Bobby Fuller's hit songs, and Steve Crosno's insatiable appetite to bring music to El Paso reveals the creativity of this era.

In their quest for rockin' sounds, they redefined space. When racist policies prevented Long John Hunter from playing in El Paso, he improvised and played from the rafters of Juárez's Lobby Bar. When Bobby Fuller and Steve Crosno were in need of recording studios, they refurbished their homes into sites of sound.

PUNK ROCK: A SONIC RECKONING OF THE 1970S

Effigies of UTEP president Joseph Smiley smoldered as three thousand students were met with tear gas on December 3, 1971. The students remained defiant and continued to march and chant, demanding that UTEP create a Chicano Studies program and hire Chicano faculty, but when the tear gas didn't work, arrests ensued. UTEP administrators had called the Texas Rangers and local law enforcement carted away thirty-four students that day.[59] The students were eventually successful, and UTEP became the first campus in the University of Texas System to launch a Chicano Studies Program.

El Paso poet Abelardo "Lalo" Delgado's "Stupid America" reveals the restive energy not only of these protests, but of the entire decade:

> stupid america, hear that chicano
> Shouting curses on the street
> he is a poet
> without paper and pencil
> and since he cannot write
> he will explode.[60]

Delgado was right. This pent-up frustration eventually detonated with fiery rebellion, both politically and culturally. After a decade of student activism and labor disputes, punk rock soon became a sonic outlet for the urgency that had been stifled for so long.

As they had been in the early twentieth century, women workers were at the forefront of insurgencies of the 1970s. At this time, El Paso was the largest jeans manufacturing city in the US, and the third largest garment manufacturing center. Farah was one such textile manufacturer that, like many other factories in El Paso, hired a predominantly Chicana workforce to work the factory floor under Anglo managers. Sexual harassment, a lack of paid sick or maternity leave, and many other labor abuses came to a head in 1972 when these Farah workers went out on strike for a union. Eventually, in 1974, Farah finally realized that they had underestimated these women and recognized their union. Although Farah eventually closed, the organizing prowess of the women continued to be vital in El Paso as they founded the activist organization La Mujer Obrera, which would play a significant role in politics and punk rock in the ensuing decade.[61]

The rebelliousness and sense of pride these students and workers exuded in many ways became the signature of this decade, not only in El Paso, but around the world, including London, UK. Across the Atlantic, the 101ers, who eventually became the iconic punk band the Clash, were cutting their teeth on a new punk sound. When Amarillo native Joe Ely met the Clash's Joe Strummer on a tour of London in 1978, Strummer confessed his love of West Texas, especially El Paso. According to Ely, "Texas was a mythical place that [the Clash] only knew about in old Marty Robbins' gunfighter ballads and Westerns and stuff." Moreover, when pondering a US tour of the United States, "the only places [Strummer] wanted to play were those he'd heard about in songs—El Paso, Laredo, and Wichita Falls."[62] This obsession eventually found its way into the Clash's music, too. In mid-1978, Strummer and Clash guitarist Mick Jones flew out to San Francisco to record tracks for the Clash's second album. El Paso's the Bobby Fuller Four's "I Fought the Law," played on the studio jukebox, and the guys were hooked. "I Fought the Law" not only became the Clash's first single released in the US, but the sound became so enmeshed with the band's signature sound that for some, like Clash bassist Paul Simonon, "I Fought the Law" became "more Clash than Bobby Fuller, really."[63]

From Carmelita Torres's brazen insurgency on the Santa Fe

Bridge to Don Tosti's "Pachuco Boogie," The Clash were tapping into a deep vein of cultural resistance coursing through Chuco. For centuries, the city and region had been a site of cultural innovation and resistance, most notably with the rise of *pachuquismo*. Style and slang had deep-rooted political significance as the efforts to suppress and eradicate the cultural influence of communities of color, especially that of Mexicans, grew in intensity. From the subversive corridos of the Mexican Revolution to the irreverent fun of Long John Hunter's "El Paso Rock," music was a formidable strain of cultural resistance that emerged from Chuco. Such relentless ingenuity went hand-in-hand with claims to space. Laws, borders, and even living room walls were disregarded in the pursuit of sound, style, and freedom. Like the Farah striking workers, this brief history illustrates how women and men, in particular Mexicanas/Chicanas, took hold of the restrictions, and bent them to serve their demands for respect and integrity. Like Carmelita Torres and her rioting comadres, they tore apart rules, regulations, and restrictions as easily as they tore apart the roofs of passing cars, simultaneously dismantling the rigid order of El Paso into the vital Chuco.

Even before The Clash's interest in the city and its deep history, youth in Chuco were already fomenting a sonic revolution by the late '70s. These chuceñas and chuceños were surging with energy to create the first wave of Chuco punk.

"ELECTRIFY ME!"

The First Wave of Chuco Punk

Surrados capitalistas
surrados capitalistas
mas bien fascistas
yo no soy fascista
soy anarquista.

The Plugz, "La Bamba," Electrify Me, *Plugz Records (1979)*

ELECTRIFY ME WAS THE PERFECT title for punk band the Plugz' first full-length release. Founded and fronted by El Paso native Tito Larriva, the sound has a classic "pop art"[1] punk sound, according to John Doe of X. It was fast-paced, cheeky, and fun. Just like Don Tosti, Larriva left Chuco for Los Angeles at an early age but never forgot about his Mexican roots. The Plugz's fifth track on the album is a cover of Richie Valens' "La Bamba," but with an appropriately punk pace that is much faster than the original version. Instead of the original chorus, the sneer of late '70s punk explodes with Larriva singing in Spanish: "Shit faced capitalists / shit faced capitalists / better yet fascist? / I am not a fascist / I am an anarchist."[2]

Although the Plugz and other Chicano punk bands in LA like the Brat, the Bags, and the Zeros, were derided as "taco punk," The Plugz and their fellow Chicano punx' hard-hitting sound was popular throughout the scene. The singular nature Larriva brought to LA and punk rock also nourished the fledgling punk scene he'd just left behind in El Paso. Indeed, Larriva's band had a particularly profound effect on a young college student named Ed Ivey. A self-described bilingual *fronterizo*, Ivey was raised on a pecan farm outside of El Paso in Clint, Texas. As a college student at UTEP majoring in journalism, he was enthralled with punk. Ivey observes, "We looked up to the Plugz because they were from El Paso, and they had integrated the Mexican sound."

As with Don Tosti, the scope and depth of Chuco's influence on music is undeniable. Historian Ricci Chávez Garcia is clear: "The Plugz' contribution to the punk scene not only established transborder Latina/o youth and culture as a prominent part of 1970s punk in Los Angeles, but also acknowledged the influential history of Latina/os in forming punk rock."[3] The sound of Don Tosti and the Plugz was both innovative and undeniably Mexican, and that sound would permeate the first wave of punk crashing down on Chuco.

While the first punx were fervently strumming the first chords of punk in El Paso, they began to reconfigure space to have punk shows that exploded along dry riverbeds and ailing airport bars. Shows were not the only focal point of this geographic disobedience. The increasing centrality of skateboarding to punk in the '80s and '90s had many of these punx carving their own thoroughfares of sound, fun, and meaning.

Community and connection were also at the core of this fledgling punk scene as they relied on one another to help with equipment and sound or to record their first records, as key Chuco punk Bobbie Welch did. In addition to punk rock, belonging and a sense of safety inspired some punx to create punk gangs, most notably, Northeast Death Squad-13, a.k.a. the NEDS. This sense of connection became especially crucial for the younger punx who were starting to go to shows and shred in local ditches. The burgeoning second generation was beginning to carve their own punk spaces throughout the city, rooted in the vitriolic punk sound of the '80s and '90s and emotional support for one another.

Second generation punk girls were finding their way to punk in different ways. A few girls found it through skateboarding, but most found it through cousins, older siblings, friends, and the local radio show *Stepping Out*, which proved foundational to their punk education.

The Plugz and the global punk revolution electrified Ivey and others in El Paso. The sound, ethos, and politics immediately energized kids along the border, and their furious creativity soon propelled them into the first wave of Chuco punk.

LAYING THE FIRST TRACKS OF THE CHUCOTOWN SOUNDTRACK

If you could get your hands on one of the few pressings of Teenage Popeye's 1981 EP, *Modern Problems*, you'd hear punk rock emerging right in El Paso at the same time that the Plugz were laying siege to Los Angeles. The frantic drum beats lure you into the first track, "Life Is Cheap," and then you are greeted with raging guitars. Gulping, David Byrne-esque singing then lays in with lyrics such as "I don't care about the oil in Iran / and I don't give a shit about Afghanistan getting invaded by the Soviets / I just want a cigarette,"[4] followed by a chorus of "Life Is Cheap." It's a fun and derisive indictment of American suburbia. *Maximum Rocknroll* described it as "cool garage punk with hilarious lyrics," but it was more than that.[5] Armed with post-punk style and scathingly sarcastic lyrics, Pierce "Chip" McDowell, Mike Nosenzo, and Johnny "Thunder" Evans of Teenage Popeye were sons of parents working at Fort Bliss. Like many punk bands of the late '70s and early '80s, they were highly political, but they also brought their experiences of living abroad to the political sensibility of the band. Teenage Popeye's sound came to the attention of more notable punk bands like the Talking Heads, and Teenage Popeye opened for them in late 1979. Although the Talking Heads held the attention of the audience and music critics, as openers, Teenage Popeye did not fly under the radar. *El Paso Times* music critic Edna Gundersen noted how the band "wipes out brain cells with two-chord thunderclaps," and cultivates a sound that, "flows from a fire-and-brimstone soapbox of omni-directional rage."⁶

Teenage Popeye's "two-chord thunderclaps" were part of El Paso's fledgling punk rock sound and culture at the time. Even though they were making it, this new music was even novel for them. First-generation Chuco punk Bobbie Welch explains, "We were really breaking ground. Punk wasn't even punk, then." Indeed, the first generation of Chuco punx like Teenage Popeye were laying the first tracks in this Chucotown soundtrack.

The Rhythm Pigs soon joined the likes of Teenage Popeye to infuse the city with sound. Although their sound was less arty than Teenage Popeye's, embracing instead the early, faster-paced hardcore punk sound of the day, the Rhythm Pigs shared Teenage Popeye's social consciousness. Tim Yohannan from *Maximum Rocknroll* described the Rhythm Pigs' sound as "highly energized" and "innovative, tight, and powerful." Their first release, *An American Activity*, began to solidify their sound and standing in punk.⁷ The album sold seven hundred copies and made *Maximum Rocknroll*'s "Alternative Top 15" in 1985. Indeed, they brought something unique to punk in the early and mid-80s, something that *MMR* termed, "Enlightened Punk." In addition to anti-militarism and pro-literacy themes, bassist and lead singer Ed Ivey's witness to animal cruelty in the area inspired his music. In 1985, he noted "[The song] 'Get it Now' is about rednecks who shoot little animals with big guns. I grew up on a farm between Clint and Fabens, and I saw people indiscriminately kill and maim animals. I'm asking in the song—if we kill animals like this, maybe, humans are next."⁸

The serious early hardcore punk of the Rhythm Pigs contrasted with what Serg Ocadiz described as "melodic, fun, sing-along punk" of the Soggy Bunz. Band members Howie "Zowie" Howard, Steve Castner, Gregg Shaw, and Serg Ocadiz added a strong dose of sonic irreverence to the Chuco sound at the time. The Soggy Bunz soon began to cultivate a reputation on tour and in El Paso for being simply irreverent and fun. Front man Ocadiz wore his mother's dresses on stage, with his hair in pigtails. Fellow band member Chickenhead would wear yoga pants and cowboy boots on stage. Their reputation as what Ocadiz refers to as "the goofy band" garnered them a strong local following. Ocadiz laughs and admits, "People liked us [but] I don't want to say it was for the music." The first tracks of this Chucotown soundtrack had a range, from the politically sardonic to the wildly absurd. By opening for bands like the Talking Heads or breaking out on MMR's "Alternative Top 15," Chuco punk was not hiding shyly in its small corner of West Texas: it was part of an emerging global punk chorus.

The diversity of Chuco's sound was also reflected in the multitude of DIY venues being developed at the time. While the Lower Valley was known for backyard shows, punk shows took place throughout the rest of the city, at failing airport bars, and even at the river's edge. Historically known as Oñate's Crossing by the old Hacienda restaurant, punx in El Paso coordinated with punx in Juárez to have free outdoor punk shows, and the only thing separating them was the dried riverbed of the Rio Grande/Río Bravo. Teenage Popeye played shows there, along with other local punk bands like the Upsets and the Rhythm Pigs. Ivey describes how at one of the Oñate's Crossing shows, the band made a deal with punx in Juárez to share their electricity. They extended a cord linked to a generator across the Rio Grande to the punx in Juárez that did not have the electricity for the show. Then, when the show started, the bands took turns playing with one another across the border. Such DIY innovation shows punx infusing derelict spaces with fun and connection.

For the scene to flourish, however, riverbeds couldn't be the only venues. To construct a lasting infrastructure of sound, the scene needed smart, dedicated, and tenacious punx with a sense of business acumen for the show to go on.

They needed someone like Bobbie Welch.

BOBBIE WELCH: ARCHITECT OF SOUND

On November 9, 1979, Bobbie Welch was helping her friends in Teenage Popeye prepare for their set. They were about to open for the Ramones. As Welch was bustling around, Joey Ramone suddenly came up to her, shook her hand, and said over and over again, "Hello,

1983 *El Paso Times* feature of punk Bobbie Welch, "Bobbie Tickets El Paso"

I am Joey Ramone. Hello, I am Joey Ramone." As a self-described "wide-eyed, punk rock girl that obviously loved music," this interaction was exciting and a bit confusing, but it was all part of the job of supporting her friends. She didn't remain star-struck for long, and soon after, she started her own label, Alien Nation. She was also the executive producer for Teenage Popeye's 1981 EP *Modern Problems*. Welch was at the eye of this punk storm, and she continued to leave a mark on punk and El Paso for decades.

Barbara Ann "Bobbie" Welch was part of a military family and had spent the early part of her life abroad before moving to El Paso at the age of sixteen. For a teenager immersed in the cultural diversity of countries like Turkey and Germany, El Paso was ideal because of the vitality she felt at her new home on the border. As the daughter of a colonel, she and the children of other military officers lived in the central part of the city, where she attended Burgess High School. There, she met the guys from Teenage Popeye. Punk rock emerged at the perfect time to feed her voracious political and intellectual appetite, as well as her desire for community. She explains, "I know a lot of people think that punk rock is just stupid people who cannot play two chords, but that's not true at all. I mean, [there were] really great discussions about everything about the world, about film. I mean, it was just a whole mélange of stuff percolating. And that's exciting to be part of."

Welch plunged into the punk rock that was "percolating" at the time. She played guitar in a couple of bands, but really found most of her focus helping her friends set up shows and booking live music. She soon combined her love of such DIY shows and punk rock with her business and organizational acumen. After finishing her degree in philosophy at UTEP, her first "real job" was working for a new business called Ticketmaster, which started in Phoenix, Arizona. One of the first Ticketmaster offices was in El Paso, where Welch cut her teeth on the dynamics of the formal music business. She recounts how she had just been "schlepping" for local bands, so when she applied, she started answering phones and selling tickets for the new business. She soon became a central point person for music and events in the region, and she caught the attention of the *El Paso Times* for her work. In 1983, an article titled "Bobbie Tickets El Paso" was the "Limelight" feature of the local newspaper. Donning a very Siouxsie and the Banshees-meets-Joan Jett look, Welch's photo accompanied an account of her leading this upstart business while helping to bring major events to the area, as a twenty-six-year-old.[9]

Despite her early success, Welch kept her toes in both the growing Ticketmaster and the up-and-coming punk rock scene. Along with local promoters Mike Jennings and Joe Dorgan, Welch successfully applied for non-profit status for the creation of Sound Seas, a local punk/alternative venue. Welch not only wrote the grant to obtain the non-profit status for Sound Seas, she also became its treasurer. Starting out downtown on Texas Street in 1984, Sound Seas eventually moved to a pig farm on the east side of the city. It became a transformative venue, where the likes of the Dead Milkmen and Suicidal Tendencies played. The Montana street Sound Seas location was eventually shut down. Recalling the closure, Soggy Bunz lead singer Serg Ocadiz said, laughing, "I don't want to say it was because [of] people peeing over the fence on pigs or anybody trying to ride a pig. [None] of us punkers [would] do that!"

Despite the trouble of playing shows on a pig farm, the combination of these three minds was very powerful. In 1987, Welch and two other women, Barbara Hubbard and Pam Smeltzer, were on the front page of the *El Paso Times* section titled "A Game Called Promotion," which profiled the women and their work to bring music and other events to the region.[10] A few pages later, the feature mentions partners Joe Dorgan, an undergrad at UTEP, and Mike Jennings, who was then earning his master's degree at UTEP. Combined with

Welch, who was a candidate for her MA in anthropology-philosophy-literary criticism, there was an extremely energetic and educated musical brain trust working to bring both major and underground acts to El Paso in the 1980s.[11] Although few women were playing in bands in this first wave of Chuco punk, women like Bobbie Welch were already very much at the helm. Welch was instrumental in rooting punk in her city by becoming one of the most notable and formidable promoters in the entire region. In 1987, Welch wanted to leave the city for the greener pastures of San Francisco, but she explained her decision to stay in a 1987 interview with the *El Paso Times*, in which she said, "I've seen so many people put blood on the line to make El Paso a better place that I'd like to continue in that effort."[12]

There was so much to put on the line, not only for Welch, but for the entire punk community, because at this time, punk was widening in scope and rocketing into so many divergent and exciting directions, even in the realm of gang activity.

THREE BLIND BATS AND DEATH SQUAD-13

The Northeast of El Paso is right next to the Fort Bliss Army Base, and historically, the surrounding area was created to cater to military enlistees. As a result, low-income housing, brothels, and speakeasies were characteristic of the area in the early twentieth century. In the 1980s and 1990s, criminal activity in the area intensified, including drugs, prostitution, and gang violence, especially in the zone known as the Devil's Triangle. According to criminologist and El Paso native Mike Tapia, crime in the Northeast had peaked around 1994, transforming this area into "one of the most gang-ridden parts of the city."[13] With the Bishops, Los Midnight Locos, and El Monte Flores, among many others dominating the Northeast, gangs had a chilling effect on Rob and Eric Schaffinos' lives in the area. Even though the two brothers had already started their new hardcore punk band Three Blind Bats, the gang harassment was so unrelenting that they began to ponder doing more than playing music.

We couldn't skate without the gangs showing up in cars or just standing there watching us. We pretty much got to a point where we could not go anywhere or do anything. My brother and I got tired of it. And so, we decided, Let's start our own gang. Starting a gang was not about being tough. It was about being able to get from point A to point B.

Teenage fantasies of forming a punk gang became a reality after an especially violent show in Northeast El Paso. Three Blind Bats and the Soggy Bunz were set to play a show at a house party, and word got out that a local neighborhood gang was going to raid the party. The bands still played, and later in the night, members of the gang jumped some of the girls at the show. The guys in the band ran outside and met the rival gang with violence. According to Schaffino, "It was total chaos," and it was this chaos which made their plans of creating a punk gang a reality.

While the proliferation of the gangs and bullying the Schaffinos faced was stifling, one of the largest gangs in El Paso, Varrio Northeast (VNE), became the stylistic model for their own gang. Rob Schaffino explains that VNE cholos often rocked out at punk shows, not to intimidate them, but because they enjoyed the music. They even got down in the pit. Schaffino also shared musical tastes with them "because the oldies, the Chuco stuff. That's our background; that's who we were, and I could relate to it so much." Their gang's name soon evolved into Northeast Death Squad and became commonly known as the NEDs. The NEDs and Three Blind Bats were recognized throughout the scene, in part because you couldn't help but notice them as they cruised through the city. They embraced a classic, signature style of black bandanas, black jeans, and black steel-toed boots.

What Rob Schaffino describes as Three Blind Bats' aggressive sound, style, and approach was a fusion of influences from Chuco and wider punk rock. Rather than punk as music and style disconnected from cultural and regional histories, they fused classic Chicano style with punk as part of their unique identities. The "Oldies Chuco" element of the NEDs style was a reflection, for example, of the music and style of their neighborhoods. Three Blind Bats created their own version of punk that embraced their roots and context.

Three Blind Bats/the NEDs' fashion and sound were not frivolous; rather, they were extraordinary tools of resistance. The NEDs and their style were part of the tradition of pachuco resistance and the contemporary punk tradition of style as power. Riot Grrrl musician and zinester Tobi Vail expressed her desire to form a gang around the same time in 1991:

> We have big plans for a grassroots, girl power, teenage girl movement of youth rebellion—jackets, we need jackets. The power of style must not be downplayed in terms of political mobilization. Can't you picture it—gangs of girls . . . girls so strong together that no one dares to fuck with them when they're walking down the street.[14]

Punk style was a powerful tool of resistance among the broader punk community where confrontations with gangs were a reality. Three Blind Bats/the NEDs are just another example of how Chuco punx recalibrated the geographic and sonic landscapes with sound and style.

Despite the existence of little to no formal research on punk gangs, it's clear that the Schaffinos' Northeast Death Squad was part of wider trends of punx forming gangs. This broader movement of punk gangs can be seen in the memoir of Black LA punk Adam Wilson. He was a member of the punk gang Sadistic Exploits in the early '80s. Even before he joined his first punk gang, others like the Los Angeles Death Squad (LADS) and their enemies from Venice Beach called Suicidal Tendencies (S.T.), led by the band's lead singer Mike Muir, were integral players in the LA punk world. These gangs were also multiracial, as Wilson describes how white, Black, and Chicanx folk found badly needed protection and connection, especially for punx without homes. While he acknowledges that people of color were not the majority in punk spaces in LA, his accounts shed light on the elemental influence of punx of color on the formation of punk gangs in the '80s/early '90s.[15]

When the Schaffinos moved to the Lower Valley, the "Northeast" part of the name was dropped, and they soon became "Death Squad 13." Although the gang was important, Rob Schaffino emphasizes that "the music was always the goal." Soon, they needed a bassist and a guitarist and needed to reach out beyond the Lower Valley to keep fueling that Three Blind Bats' sound.

Close friend Gabriela Díaz, who was from the West Side of town, in Canutillo, became a key point of connection between the Schaffinos in the Lower Valley and younger punx on the West Side. Díaz became involved in the punk community because her mom and cousin owned a restaurant across from Hanks High School on the East Side. Due to the proximity to the high school, local punx asked to have shows there, and the owners obliged. Two of the bands that played at this restaurant were the Organ Donors and the Soggy Bunz, and Díaz was in the audience. For Díaz, the energetic sound and feeling of punk was liberating because of the acceptance and belonging the community provided. Hooked on that sense of belonging, she soon started going to other local punk shows, like one at Coronado High School in 1988 where she met fourteen-year-old West Side punk and future ATDI front man Cedric Bixler-Závala. Díaz eventually introduced Bixler-Závala to Rob Schaffino, who was looking for a bassist. Although Bixler-Závala had been singing for the band Phantasmagoria, this mixture of hardcore punk band/gang was too intoxicating of an elixir to resist for Bixler-Závala. He left his old band and soon became the bassist for Three Blind Bats. For Rob Schaffino, the addition of Cesar Mendez on guitar and Bixler-Závala on bass meant Three Blind Bats were sounding better than ever.

With Bixler-Závala in the band, the Schaffinos began making their mark in their new area of town. One way to do this was to race around the Lower Valley in Rob Schaffino's '56 Chevy. Years later, the front man recalled these excursions in "Schaffino," one of the songs on ATDI's first LP, *Acrobatic Tenement:*

Racing by in a '56 Chevy
And we couldn't even pretend
To be alive
To be alive[16]

Three Blind Bats/Death Squad 13 mobilized to reclaim space for skaters, punx, and punk rock fans, but they were not the only ones. Punx were putting on shows at restaurants, where Gabriela Díaz found both sound and a comforting feeling of belonging with punx throughout the city.

Rather than copying punx in the UK, El Paso punx created a style and sound that reflected the homegrown Mexican roots of the city. Kids of color like the Scaffinos and Díaz were key creators of punk rock from its emergence, and they were not alone. Punx of color in cities like Los Angeles were engaging in punk gang culture just like in Chuco. Chuco was no outlier, but part of the broader creation of punk rock culture.

Three Blind Bats were especially foundational to this first wave of Chuco punk, but also instrumental in nurturing the impending second wave, with Bixler-Závala in tow. This mixing of punk generations was not unique to Three Blind Bats. Out on the streets, older and younger skate punx were carving, kickflipping, and ollieing together.

Skateboarding was propelling Chuco punk forward into the second wave.

RUNWAYS FOR THE NEW GENERATION OF PUNK ROCK

Footage of Uglor's 1988 show at the El Paso skate ditch known as "Three Fountains" still exists. The VHS-converted footage captures the band playing almost indifferently in front of an orange van against the sun-bleached El Paso skyline. Uglor's bare-chested lead singer sings little and mainly mills about as the guitarist, in a cut-off Misfits' t-shirt, and the drummer, obscured by his drum kit, drives the gnarly chords and beats. The late-teens, early-twenties crowd is a snapshot of late '80s style, Joey Belladonna and Dave Mustaine semi-mullets and

Serg Ocadiz of the Soggy Bunz playing at the "Project Graduation" celebration at Western Playland, 1988

the smattering of girls in oversized Debbie Gibson T-shirts tucked into billowing shorts.

But the majority of Uglor's expectant audience look to be thirteen- to fifteen-year-old skate boys with shaved heads save for their long bangs, holding their decks as they wait for the sound to explode. After ten minutes, the music finally starts to snarl and gain momentum, and these previously aloof pre-pubescent skaters begin to propel them- selves into a moshing frenzy.[17] Part of this preteen mix was a young Cedric Bixler-Závala. Decades later, he remembers:

> I went to a ditch called "Three Fountains" where we all hung out and skated. . . . Uglor was playing by chance, and they had a generator, and someone even filmed it. So I actually have proof of my first punk show. I'm in there, trying to slam dance.[18]

The fusion of punk and skateboarding are obvious at the show, and so too is the merging of the first generation of Chuco punx such as the band Uglor and the second generation of mainly boys like Bix-ler-Závala. Punk historian David A. Ensminger explains, "Skateboard-ing is a crucial link between the era of the 1960s post-Beat Generation and the Punks. . . . The sport connects the dots between a Beat sense of spontaneous possibility . . . and Do-It-Yourself attitude/ethos of punk."[19] The links are several, and the use of skateboarding to trans-form space is one of them. Writer and cultural historian Iain Bor-den argues that skateboarding uses movement/performance instead of words to communicate with a significant effect on geography. For Borden, "Skateboarding challenges the notion that cities are to be res-olutely obeyed, that we exist solely as passive dwellers."[20] El Paso skat-ers refused to obey designated limits and uses of the city, recasting it instead into a noisier and more creative Chuco.

Ditches and skate crews forged another key link between punk rock and skating: They were sites of community, and, at times, emo-tional support that many of these boys lacked at home. The scarcity of girls at the Uglor show was not a one-off, but part of a broader development of a more male-dominated skate culture throughout the United States. Artist-Researcher Dani Abulhawa argues in *Skate-boarding and Femininity: Gender, Space-Making, and Expressive Movement* that, historically, skateboarding had become gender-limited by the '80s and '90s. For Abulhawa, street skating shared the punk "anti-social and anti-authoritarian mentality," which fused with a level of "hetero-masculinity" that objectified or denigrated anybody and anything associated with femininity.[21] At that time, it would have been rare indeed to see any girls carving along the streets and ditches of the city.

In November 1978, Terry McChesney spotted a ditch along High-way 54 in Northeast El Paso that had just been filled with concrete. For McChesney, this was the ideal spot for a "little skate park," so he built a wall, coping, two roll-ins, and a rail. McChesney named this monument to skating "the Worm," and it became the breeding ground for millions of ollies and kickflips while tightening skate punk's hold on El Paso. Soggy Bunz punx Serg Ocadiz and his friend and band-mate Howie "Zowie" Howard further illustrate how inextricably interconnected skateboarding was and is with punk, friendship, and community. According to Ocadiz, "The punk music came with the skateboards." Ocadiz was constantly building skate ramps at his friends' homes, and punk rock was the perfect soundtrack for carving and grinding. As he puts it, "That was the draw, the punk rock, the aggression of kind of like do what you want. It was fun to skate to."

The first generation of punx were soon sharing the Worm with the up-and-coming second generation. West Sider Jim Ward made clear that even for this second generation, "Skateboarding and punk back then were intertwined."[22] The most obvious points of convergence were skate compilations that featured "skate rock," much of which was punk. These comps introduced punk music to a generation of skaters. Lower Valley punk Tony Leal never skated as well as his friends like Ernesto Ybarra and Mikey Morales, but it didn't matter, because music became his focus. Leal's thrill became making the most awesome mixtapes to play while he and his friends were bombing through Chuco. He admits that eventually, his favorite part of skating was "being excited to bring new tapes of music I had discovered or a mixtape I'd be proud to show my homies."

While music was a key connection, punk and skateboarding provided a space for boys to be different and to support one another. Young Lower Valley punk Fill Heimer explains, "I was really an awkward kid, but with skating, it didn't matter." Heimer skated with others like him, including Ernesto Ybarra, Surge Mendoza, Mikey Morales, Pancho Mendoza, and Tony Leal. They eschewed basketball courts and football fields and instead charged through the city with an array of kickflips and ollies. They hung out at local sites like Rojas Ditch. Skateboarding not only opened a space for these young guys to fit in, but it also delivered powerful and lasting emotional connections. Mikey Morales notes how he and his friends would skate all over the city and have fun, but also talk and bond. He explains:

> Of course, we talked about girls. But we also talked about our strained relationships with our families. All of us seemed to be subject to a lot of verbal and emotional abuse, which turned

physical amongst a few of us within [our] households. We got blamed for everything at our homes. That was a common ground we shared. These guys were also the first people with whom I was open about my mom's schizophrenia, and they were all supportive. They were also the first friends I had sleep over. I gave them the mental prep before coming over, but it was really awesome. I finally had a support system.

Sociological and psychological research shows that young men need emotional outlets and support, and that the role of friendships cannot be overestimated. Skateboarding and punk facilitated a community for likeminded kids and paved the way for lasting friendships.[23]

This community, however, was still largely closed to girls. Before the 2001 documentary *Dogtown and Z-Boys* immortalized the myth of So-Cal guys (plus Peggy Oki) developing transition and street skating when they couldn't surf, the freestyle style of skating in the '60s and '70s more prominently included women. Freestyle involved flatland tricks like handstands and pirouettes, which could have been framed as a more appealing or more appropriate form of physical activity for women and girls. As street skating developed in the late '70s and '80s, freestyle skating was seen with disdain in the culture. Iain Borden argues that freestyle was seen as "skateboarding's feminine or homosexual 'other,' with its emphasis on grace and technique contrasting with the overt risk-taking of much transition and street skating."[24]

Only two of the eighteen punx interviewed for this book who identify as women discussed in detail their experiences as skaters. Deana Montoya's interest in skateboarding began at an early age while she lived in San Diego. At eight years old, she started to watch and photograph the neighborhood kids building boards, applying grip tape to their decks, and then skating on ramps. When her family moved to Central El Paso, skating was lonely as she carved the streets and hills on her own, but by the time she started high school on the East Side, she finally found a skate crew. Montoya declares, "You name it, we skated it!"

On the West Side, Martha Yvette Martínez's older sister was a serious skater, so even though she saw herself as more of a "girly girl" who really liked to roller skate, she also shredded on her deck. Martínez's uncle also owned Skate City, one of the skate shops in town. Her uncle even had a half pipe that she, her older sister, and her brother would skate. While Abulhawa emphasizes the lack of gender diversity in skateboarding in the '70s and '80s, she also notes that "the 1990s was the decade . . . female skateboarders [entered] into the hallowed street skating realm."[25] Montoya and Martínez can be seen as harbingers of the increased presence of Chuceñas in skateboarding.

Like the ocean waves that inspired Z-Boy skater Peggy Oki, the first generation of punx were overlapping with the second generation at places like Three Fountains, the Worm, and Rojas Ditch. Not only were these punx molding restricted and defined areas of El Paso into open gateways to fun in Chuco, they were also forging essential pillars of emotional support and growth for boys who didn't have that at home. As open as these sites were, gender did pose a limit, as the historical pattern of street skating became more male-dominated, but it did not deter girls like Montoya and Martínez from charging out on their own as they carved more solidarity and thoroughfares of fun and enjoyment.

The sounds of their wheels, bearings, and trucks barreling through their city was not punx' only noise. By the early '90s, the voices of this second generation were increasing in number and volume. They were so loud that they were shifting the gravity of punk rock to the Lower Valley, the West Side, and Juárez.

THE CENTER OF GRAVITY SHIFTS: THE LOWER VALLEY

The shift of punk energy to the Lower Valley in Southeast El Paso in many ways refocuses the importance of the area historically. After the Pueblo Revolt of 1680, the Tiguas founded Ysleta del Sur, which became the oldest town in Texas, the seat of El Paso county before it moved to El Paso, and the locus of what is known as the Lower Valley.[26] By the nineteenth century, the political and economic heft of the area began to decline for residents who were predominantly Indigenous and Mexican. In the early twentieth century, garment manufacturers

Lower Valley Punx, from left to right: Carlos Palacios, Ernesto Ybarra, Pablo Novelas, and Johnny Rios

saw the land as ideal for cultivating cotton, and Mexican workers from El Paso's Segundo Barrio and from Mexico came to work in the fields by the 1920s and 1930s. Cotton fields and a predominantly Indigenous and Mexican population increasingly characterized the area.[27]

After the Second World War, garment manufacturers left the higher paid and unionized workforce in the Northeast and the Midwest for the low wage, highly feminized workforce in the Southwest. This was particularly the case for jeans manufacturers who established themselves in El Paso in the 1960s and 1970s, transforming the city into the "blue jeans capital of the world."[28] Women in the city's Lower Valley were especially important to the growth of this industry, and punx Ernesto Ybarra and Eddie Martínez both had mothers who worked in these local Levi's factories at the time.

Families in the region were struggling, and these jobs were badly needed. The father of Lower Valley punk, Tony Leal, is a case in point. Leal's father, Antonio, worked at the Tony Lama's factory on the East

Side of El Paso during the day and then immediately went to his second job at Cowtown Boot factory for a night shift. Despite the growth in this industry at the time, layoffs were also common. Eight years into Antonio's tenure at Tony Lama, there was a massive layoff, but he was one of the "lucky ones" as he was able to keep his job if he took a massive pay cut. Leal remembers, "Those layoffs at the factories really shook some hard working family's worlds up! I was a little kid back then but could recognize when the folks were scrambling to keep things stable."

In 1986, *MMR* writer Mykel Board claimed that "Punk comes from the land of shopping malls and cloned split-level houses. It doesn't come from the crumbling walls of the burnt-out city."[29] However, Ybarra, Martínez, and Leal's class backgrounds, along with many other Chuco punx, particularly from the Lower Valley, were firmly working class. Even if there were shopping malls nearby, they were also close to Levi's factories and cotton fields where their families toiled. This sense of ethnic and class consciousness eventually infused the identity of the first bands of second wave Lower Valley Chuco punk, bands like Not So Happy. The working-class and largely Mexican and Indigenous community would fuel this punk revolution.

Not So Happy was the brainchild of Surge Mendoza and Ernesto Ybarra, but it was also a product of the area and circumstance. As young kids, Surge and Ybarra were already skateboarding around the Lower Valley and going to heavy metal backyard shows. The teenagers did not look down on these young punx; rather, they invited the two youngsters to jam out with them. The two had yet to form their own band, but that would happen soon. Surge recounts the moment when goofing around with Ybarra on guitar finally coalesced into their first band. That day, they happened to skate by Alex Martínez's house, who was hosting a Lower Valley backyard punk show. Identifying them as a potentially receptive audience, Martínez invited them into the show. Ybarra then lied to Martínez and told him that he and Surge had a band and were happy to play a show at Martínez's house. Martínez agreed.

There was no band.

In proper DIY fashion, Ybarra and Surge now had to put one together. They eventually found a drummer, Pudge, who had been playing Mexican music in his dad's Mexican band. Three days later, hardcore punk band Not So Happy played their first show to about thirty people in Martínez's backyard. Even though they could warm themselves with fires in barrels at the show, the winter cold made the show all the more difficult, and the newly formed band spent most of the time in their truck with the motor running and random punx sticking their hands in the truck for warmth. Despite this challenging first show, they were hooked and eventually went out on their first tour. When their first drummer was no longer able to play, Lower Valley punk Mikey Morales took to the drums.

Almost immediately, Ybarra connected with Devon Morph from punk monthly zine *Maximum Rocknroll*, and the new band was featured in the 1993 issue. The working-class lives of these Lower Valley punx is apparent in the interview. Morales said, "It's weird, yeah, there's all these rich kids that have this mindset, 'We're more punk than you' because they can buy more things. They've got money, they flaunt it around, they get all these tapes and stuff. It's like whatever." Bandmate Ybarra added, "With their hundred-dollar Doc Martens, you know they haven't been in the scene because they're are all new faces. They think they're more punk than you because they all have more shit."[30]

Although lacking in economic resources, Lower Valley punx had family and community to support this nascent scene. For many, grandparents and parents actively encouraged their sonic longings. For instance, Morales' neighbor and childhood friend, Carlos Palacios, fed Morales' musical talent and passion. For Palacios, Morales was and is "like a brother," so when Morales needed a drum kit he could not afford, Rosa Palacios, Carlos' mother, gave Morales her drum kit.

The most legendary supporter in the Lower Valley, however, was Patricia "Pat" or "Patty" Youngblood's Blood Management, which managed Lower Valley punk bands, including her son's band, Faction X. From the late 1980s to 1993, in addition to Faction X, Patty Youngblood managed other bands like Not So Happy, Spoiled Milk, Stressed Out, and Aggressor. Although she was booking her bands and out-of-town bands like Naked Aggression, the nefarious and threatening names belied a very altruistic motivation.

When her son Jay wanted to start Faction X with his friends, Patty was not surprised. She herself was a music major at UTEP at the time and had been playing guitar in local clubs for fifteen years. That inspired Jay to take up the guitar himself, and when he wanted to play in his own band, Pat thought it best to put her knowledge of the music business to work and manage many of these up-and-coming Lower Valley punk bands. In the 1993 edition of *Book Your Own Fuckin' Life* (a yearly catalog of punk, underground, and DIY resources which had started out in the back pages of *Maximum Rocknroll*), while other promoters, venues, and bookstores in Texas had aloof and ironic names like "No Talent" and "Splatter Fest," Youngblood did not shy away from revealing a sincere enthusiasm for booking:

> Patty Youngblood
> Hi! Give me a call or write if you'd like to play in El Paso. Send a promo pack and contact me at least one month in advance, so I can make the necessary arrangements.
> Thanx![31]

In the same issue was Ed Ivey's ad, revealing his transition from lead singer of the Rhythm Pigs to promoter of the younger generation of punx.

> Ed Ivey
> Venues, various from hall shows to small cafe shows. Lodging: floor crash, or cheap hotel rooms. Food: will provide hot Mexican food & beverages, but bands must supply their own booze if they choose. Working terms: usually small guarantee plus % of net receipts.[32]

Patty Youngblood and Ivey nurtured this rich milieu of young punx that was blossoming throughout the city, especially in the Lower Valley. Indeed, their participation, along with the support of people like Carlos Palacios' mother, Rosa Palacios, underscores how punk rock participation transcended playing drums or guitar on stage: it also involved supporting your *hitos* so they could take the stage in the first place.

While Blood Management was an essential part of the Lower Valley scene, young punx were already starting to book their own shows as well, especially Faction X bassist Alex Martínez. Martínez recounts one of the first shows he booked in a vacant lot across from his house. He had booked the Connecticut bands Brutally Familiar and The Pips. Although one of his first shows, it was a huge success. According to Martínez, the mosh pits were so immense, they created a "dust storm." "They really rocked hard," he said. "They had the cholos going crazy, too." This crazy show in a vacant lot was the apogee of punx taking what was abandoned space and filling it with sound and meaning, thereby defying the boundaries of El Paso and twisting them into the more vibrant Chuco.

The entryway into this second generation of punk was not always as open as the vacant lot that Martínez turned into a punk venue. Sometimes, the entry points were closer to home.

As a middle schooler, Lower Valley punk Sophia Orquiz loved to listen to Joe Dorgan's radio show *Stepping Out,* where she got the chance to listen to bands like Joy Division, Ministry, the Pet Shop Boys, and Jane's Addiction. The show came on late in the evening, so she would have to furtively play it at a very low volume to prevent her mother from getting after her for not going to bed.

Orquiz's rocking subterfuge in many ways reveals the gendered nature of punk entry. Not that boys weren't secretly hunkered down to listen to punk also, but for the women/queer punx I interviewed, the process occurred in more private, rather than public spaces. These more private routes to punk align with the theories of cultural studies scholar Angela McRobbie, who scoffed at subcultural theorists' frustration at not being able to find the girls. For McRobbie, the girls were not absent; they simply faced more barriers to accessing public spaces where researchers identified youth subcultures. Finding girls in subcultures involved shifting one's gaze "to the terrain of domestic life . . .

if we wanted to know about teenage femininity or about female youth culture."[33]

One of those more domestic and personal sites was close friendships. While playing in bands was a key connection to this Lower Valley scene, there were a variety of different entry points or hooks into punk rock that were highly gendered. Lindy Hernández, for example, didn't even know the differences among genres when she was young, so she listened to hip-hop as well as bands like the Cure and Violent Femmes. Even her first shows, the Chicano rap of Lighter Shade of Brown and Kid Frost, were not punk rock. Friendship, however, proved one central opening into punk for Hernández and her best friend Erica Ortegón. Ortegón describes how the two girls "discovered punk and the punk scene together." The music and ethics were the initial draw to the sound, revealing the types of bonds that forged the intimate scaffolding to create a vibrant punk scene for girls.

Feminist politics were another route to punk. Franko Tormenta was born in El Paso but grew up in Juárez. He started living with his grandparents in the Lower Valley where he attended elementary school. Going to school and speaking Spanish, combined with having to move at an early age, was difficult for Tormenta. Mistreatment was common from others on another level, because people recognized from early on that he was gay. Music became a way to find a space of acceptance, a common struggle among LGBTQ youth even today. However, he did not find refuge and support with skaters in middle school; rather, he says his closest friends were cholas and "rocker chicks" who listened to heavy metal. He liked the anger of heavy metal, but the homophobia and sexism were a turnoff. For him, the movie *Lola La Trailera* was much more inspiring of his feminism that was "primal" and not "academic." He says he saw men in his neighborhood "just beating the fuck out of women," and since he felt he was treated like a woman, he had a strong affinity for feminism and eventually punk rock.

Despite the prevailing narrative of punk being the exclusive domain of middle class white kids, the punk rock dynamism brewing in the Lower Valley of El Paso was solidly Brown and working-class.

To understand Chuco punk, we must understand the family and community that allowed them to thrive. In their rush to make noise, Lower Valley punx were nourished by family members like Rosa Palacios and Patty Youngblood, as well as older punx.

Lower Valley punx were indeed thriving, with bands like Faction X and Not So Happy throwing shows in backyards and abandoned lots, reclaiming space for the rowdy and creative Chuco. For girls and queer punx, their conduits into punk rock were more private, but no less powerful. These second-generation women and queer punx were part of this transformation of space into Chuco, but they were starting from a more intimate place.

Across town, their peers on the West Side were similarly voracious as they sought to satiate their punk appetites.

THE WEST SIDE

The solidly working-class and Mexican Lower Valley scene emerged simultaneously with the burgeoning West Side scene, but the two scenes were a study in contrasts. Contemporary statistics illustrate the stark differences. In 2022, the median household income of West Side residents was approximately $74,000 a year, with only 68 percent of the residents identifying as Hispanic.[34] On the other hand, Hispanics made up 95 percent of Lower Valley residents and had a median household income of $32,000 a year.[35] The punx from El Paso High School, including Beto O'Rourke, Cedric Bixler-Závala, and Jim Ward represent the more middle-to-upper class and ethnically diverse character of the area. The lives of punx like Gabe González, Jessica Flores, and Omar Rodríguez-López, on the other hand, show that poverty and racism were rife on the West Side, too.

González started playing guitar at the age of seven and was in a band by age thirteen. The excitement of punk was a definite draw, and his first tour with the band Spindrift at the age of fifteen saw him end up in Seattle, even though he was supposed to be sleeping over at his friend's house in El Paso. However, this punk, teenage rebellion had

West Side Punk Barry Peterson

roots in his family history and the broader history of inequality on El Paso's West Side. His father's family was from Smeltertown, a company town built around the American Smelting and Refining Company (ASARCO) in 1887 in Northwest El Paso. Segregated by race and occupation, El Alto, the upper region, housed Anglo managers, and El Bajo, the lower region, was where Mexican and Black workers like González's grandfather and uncle lived. Approximately 2,500 people resided in Smeltertown, forging a proud and tight-knit community around their place of work. Yet, the most formidable challenge they faced had everything to do with the emissions spewing out of the iconic ASARCO smokestack: lead poisoning. The problem became so severe that by the early 1970s, 43 percent of all age groups and 62 percent of children ten years old and younger living within a one-mile radius of the smelter were found to have lead blood levels eight times what the CDC recommends today.[36] Although public outcry over the pollution and health effects led to the eviction of Smeltertown residents in 1972, the legacy of the town, the community, and the suffering of his family is still poignant for González, who was born two years after the demise of Smeltertown. As a teenager the angst that fueled his passion for music emerged from seeing family members suffer from ASARCO-related sicknesses and, at times, their struggles paying for medications to treat those ailments.

Fellow West Side punk Jessica Flores was also deeply affected by her family's connection to Smeltertown. According to Flores, "Smeltertown has always been a big part of [her] history," and it is the key reason why she grew up on the West Side of El Paso. Flores had familial connections to Smeltertown on both sides of her family, and her family has been active in commemorating the factory town, or *colonia*, since she was a kid. Her grandfather, in particular, was active in organizing golf tournaments and Smeltertown reunions. Flores explains, "My grandpa was very proud to be from Smeltertown, to have worked at ASARCO and be a part of it. [Smeltertown residents] had to have this sense of community to feel good about where they came from." Living on the more affluent West Side, however, made her experience with poverty all the more painful, leaving a space for punk rock to fill. Flores reflects "The music . . . had a lot of aggression at the time. . . . 1990s punk, especially underground punk at the time [had] a lot of anger and aggression, and that just suited [me] at the time with the trouble I was going through in my own life." For both González and Flores, punk rock was an essential outlet for their frustration with racial and class injustice. Their shared focus on and memory of their Smeltertown roots—a place that had been physically destroyed—illustrates their effort to forge a Chuco that embraces historic and cultural sites of significance like those in Smeltertown.

Although from a relatively more affluent family, future At the Drive-In guitarist Omar Rodríguez-López's experiences with racism were especially profound. As a kid, he experienced racist bullying after his family left Puerto Rico for South Carolina, where "friends" who called him "spic" would gaslight him by telling him that the word meant "cool guy." Even though his family settled in the predominantly Mexican El Paso, the pressure to assimilate to white culture was still alienating, but punk became an outlet, and that outlet started a riot.[37]

By the beginning of the '90s, this generation of punx had started a sonic coup d'etat in Chuco. At a punk show at Coronado High School in 1991, another one of Rodríguez-López's bands, Startled Calf, was the focal point of the so-called Coronado High School Riot.

ANARCHY ON THE WEST SIDE: THE CORONADO HIGH SCHOOL "RIOT" OF '91

Lower Valley punk Jacob Trevizo remembers his friend Dino inviting him to a "battle of the bands thing at Coronado [High School]," and since the band Strange Mary from Hanks High School in East El Paso were playing, it was "going to be an epic showcase." Trevizo agreed to go, so they headed out in Dino's old Dodge Torino to the West Side. What started off as a "Save the Environment" benefit show in the Coronado High School gym, turned into an intergenerational conflict when kids started indulging in adolescent anarchy. If you can stand to follow the shaky and dark Camcorder video of the December 14, 1991, benefit for more than a few minutes, you'll see Rodríguez-López spring up and shout, just as his band, Startled Calf comes down with beats and chords. What ensues is known as "The Coronado High School Riot."[38] In that crowd was Central El Paso punk Dave Acosta, who saw a flyer for the show at the Headstand, so he and his friend took off to the West Side. When they arrived, Acosta was shocked at the turnout. "Everybody was there," he says. "Everyone I had seen at shows. Oh shit! Cedric is here. Ralph Hasso. I didn't know who Omar was then, but I remember when Startled Calf came out, I was like, 'Who's this little dude? Oh, he's like another Cedric, crazy.' There was already a lot of slam dancing. People started stage diving during Startled Calf." Staff stepped in and grabbed Rodríguez-López, then put a stop to the show; supposedly Rodríguez-López would not give up the mic, and security had to wrestle the mic from him. From Acosta's point of view, "That's what triggered the quote unquote riot, which was really everyone yelling [for security] to leave Omar [Rodríguez-López] alone, and [then security] kicking everybody out of the gym." As the kids filed out, their youthful snark found expression in the parking lot as they burst out singing Christmas carols to antagonize the staff putting an end to the show.

Even if the show wasn't much of a riot, it signaled the frenzy of punk activity. While the West Side was very different from the Lower Valley, the punx there struggled with many of the same issues. Rodríguez-López's struggles with racism and Jessica Flores' frustration with the affluence of the area represent Brown and working-class struggles and contributions to punk rock.

These experiences fueled their love for punk as bands like Spindrift and Startled Calf became a ferocious outlet to express their pain. The sound inspired them to roam as far as Seattle, and to reinvent spaces for stage diving and punk festivals. West Side punx were wrestling control of docile spaces like the Coronado High School gym from authorities and forging them into fiery spaces of sound and rebellion that were integral to forging Chuco and its soundtrack.

These punk fires in the Lower Valley and West Side could never burn in isolation. Juárez and El Paso are known as las ciudades gemelas (twin cities). They are intimately intertwined.

Across the international border, punx were scrambling to find their own sound, too.

PUNK EN LA CIUDAD GEMELA

All the fun was not confined to El Paso. There were young kids with a blossoming desire for music and disorder in Juárez, too. Indeed, for decades, Juárez was bigger and more at the cutting edge of culture. While El Paso did build the exquisite Alhambra Theater in the early twentieth century, which showed one of the first color motion pictures in Texas (and a century later become the site of Tricky Falls), for instance, Teatro Juárez was far more advanced with its phonograph that synchronized with films. Juárez was also the center of jazz. During Prohibition, Americans not only flocked to Juárez for liquor, they also crossed the bridges in hopes of tapping into the refined jazz culture.[39] Later in the '60s, it was where you could find Long John Hunter hanging from the rafters in the Lobby Bar. By the 1990s, Juárez continued to overshadow her twin, El Paso, with a population of around 798,499 in 1990, much bigger than El Paso's 591,610 residents.[40] The drive and creativity to surface in Juárez, and from other cities in Mexico, should not come as a surprise. The international border would not form a rigid demarcation; rather, familial and historic connections between El Paso and different parts of Mexico, especially cities in Chihuahua, ensured a steady flow of musical creativity that transcended national borders.

Punk Edmundo "Mundo" Valencia, for instance, spent the first years of his life in Mexico City, but then moved to the Lower Valley and lived right near Mikey Morales and Carlos Palacios in the Lower Valley of El Paso. Rosa Palacios was good friends with Mundo's mother. When she tried to get the boys to play together, Mundo only spoke Spanish, and Carlos only spoke English, so early connections were difficult. Mundo was also shy, so he would watch as Mikey and Carlos skated around town. As he got older, he fell in love with music, and the first shows he saw were rock shows in Juárez. He did not always have to go to Juárez to see the *rock en español* shows. In 1993, Mexican bands Maldita Vecindad y Los Hijos del Quinto Patio and Caifanes played at Kendall Hall at UTEP campus. Valencia remembers, "Oh, and of course, it was like a theater format with the seating for theater people. . . . Of course, people didn't sit down. Of course not. I mean, it was slam dancing. People were pulling seats off the floor. I'm not kidding." Even at a young age, Mundo revealed the fluidity of the border and the relationships that flowed throughout it.

More than two hundred miles away in Cd. Chihuahua, Gaspar Orozco was listening to his parents' Rolling Stones and Bob Dylan albums. By the sixth grade, he had started to be attracted to the sounds of heavy metal, but he came to see punk as more political and as a type of music that attacked what he saw as social and political injustice that was rife in the world. He eventually found a natural sonic home in the music of the Clash, the Exploited, and the Dead Kennedys. His family vacations to El Paso were also formative. Observing the struggles of undocumented Mexicans crossing into the United States was especially powerful for him.

Although young Orozco's ideas about immigration justice were just beginning to evolve, his criticism was rooted in the reality and current events taking place in El Paso. First, it wasn't until the late 1970s that the US Border Patrol began to hire Hispanics. Second, in this era the Border Patrol had a policy of capturing undocumented peoples after they crossed the border, an effort that upper administration in the Border Patrol emphasized to justify annual budgets. This tactic was particularly dehumanizing to both undocumented peoples and natives of El Paso. *El Paso Times* journalist Leticia Zamarripa interviewed one Border Patrol Officer in 1996 who admitted, "Chasing people is part of the Border Patrol mystique. That's our heritage. I used to love what I did for a living."[41]

Such "mystique" and "heritage" came with abuses, too. For instance, in the 1980s, the Border Patrol was also known to purposely leave holes in the fences along the border with Mexico so agents could follow the flow of undocumented peoples traveling through and apprehend them once they were in El Paso. The Border Patrol also had a regular presence on Bowie High School's campus in Segundo Barrio, a strategy to catch undocumented peoples as soon as they stepped foot on American soil. In May of 1992, a Border Patrol agent stopped a visually impaired Mexican American Bowie High School student on his way home from graduation rehearsal. When the student evoked his right not to answer the agent's questions and attempted to walk away, the agent threw the student up against a fence, roughed him up, spat in his face, and threatened him with further violence before allowing him to leave. The student eventually contacted the Border Rights Coalition, a local human rights advocacy group that had already been amassing similar reports of the Border Patrol's abuses throughout El Paso. In October of 1992, this student's report became part of *Murillo v. Musegades*, a massive federal lawsuit against the Border Patrol which ultimately forced them to stop harassing students based on their race and reconfigured enforcement along the Mexico-United States border.[42]

While Border Patrol agents and government officials were seeking to make the international border less porous and more rigid, both Valencia and Orozco reveal how it still constituted a shared cultural landscape. Whether it was Valencia watching rock and punk shows on both side of the border or the righteous anger Orozco's trips up north had inspired, the area continued to be fluid, nourishing these two punx' desire for sound.

Juárez would play a significant role in Chuco punk. In particular, while "El Paso" and "Juárez" are official designations separated by an international border, the Chuco where pachucos emerged from both sides of the border presages the wild, irreverent Chuco punk that ignored such borders in the quest for sound and connection.

The countervailing energies only intensified as this second generation of punx matured.

"I'M PLANNING A BIG SURPRISE"

Lower Valley punk Erik Frescas was a freshman in high school when he pressed play on his Walkman to hear Fugazi's new release *13 Songs* for the first time. Joe Lally's bassline introduced "Waiting Room," and a moment in time was crystalized for Frescas. "It was really that moving and life changing. And to this day, I remember exactly where I was at in my life when I hit play."

"Waiting Room" was transformative for Frescas, and it embodies the restless tenor of the Chuco scene at this time. The Rhythm Pigs had already moved to San Francisco. No longer the "wide-eyed punk rock girl," Bobbie Welch was a major promoter who had brought U2 with openers Public Enemy and the Sugarcubes to El Paso in 1992. Bobbie Welch reveals the ever-present role of women in Chuco punk. Welch was, and is, everywhere. Like air and gravity, women might prove less visible, but Welch and future punkeras will show that they are elemental. Moreover, Welch's meteoric rise was indicative of how she and her generation of punx were charging away in different directions, leaving shoes to fill back home that these up-and-coming punx like Frescas were eager to fill.

By the early '90s, both first and second generation punx had reclaimed spaces from pig farms to high school gyms and bent them into the service of punk sound and community, thereby re-creating Chuco. In addition to creating feisty and fiery music, they sought belonging and focus, which they found with one another. Whether it was carving through "The Worm" or watching *Lola La Trailera*, punx found different avenues into punk that were shaped by gender, gender-identity, and sexuality. The central role Brown, working class punx played in these two waves of Chuco punk further affirms that Chicanas and Chicanos were integral architects of punk rock sound and culture.

In the song "Waiting Room," Ian MacKaye conveys an impatience, a restlessness that these young Chuco punx were consumed with by the early '90s. Carlos Palacios remembers by the time he was done with middle school, his attitude was: "Fuck it all! I want to play in punk bands and set up shows!"

Palacios was not alone; he was part of this second wave of punx that was not, as Ian MacKaye extols in "Waiting Room," going to "sit idly by," and who were ready to release this ferocious, unrelenting energy and sound on their city.

They had a big surprise in store for Chuco.

"RASCUACHE"

The "Second Generation" Finds Its Sound

> Radiate this frequency and show me just what the hell you mean.
>
> *At the Drive-In, "Rascuache," Vaya, Fearless Records, 1999*

> The Do-It-Yourself sensibility at the core of punk musical subcultures found resonance with the practice of rasquache, a Chicana/o cultural practice of "making do" with limited resources.
>
> *Michelle Habell-Pallán,* Loca Motion: The Travels of Chicana and Latina Popular Culture, *2005*

> Rascuache [is] the term for making something from readily available materials. An old tire transformed into a planter. A shed patched with hubcaps. A toy airplane made from a beer can. Poverty is the mother of invention.
>
> *Sandra Cisneros, "Que Vivan Los Colores!" in* A House of My Own: Stories from My Life, *2015*

"HERE COME THE PICAS!" ERICA Ortegón's little nephew screamed, referring to the throngs of Liberty Spikes and Mohawks as punx charged into her Lower Valley backyard for yet another show. While shows along riverbeds and in high school gyms continued to be outposts of this ferocious punk ingenuity, Lower Valley backyard shows

Rocking at the Arboleda House. Lindy Hernández and Erica Ortegón are pictured with members of the punk band Bristle.

composed the nexus of live music culture for the second generation, and Ortegón's backyard was a pivotal part of it. Indeed, her backyard became such a widely known venue that punx throughout the city simply called it the "Arboleda House."

To provide electricity for the bands playing in the backyard at the Arboleda House, Ortegón ran an extension cord through her mother's bedroom and connected the cord to the wall outlet, which made the shows all the more precarious. She remembers that during one show, she had left the connection of the cord to someone else who, instead of connecting it to her mother's bedroom, connected it to the bathroom light. She explains, "So the band would be playing; everyone's getting excited, and someone would use the bathroom or turn off the light, and then the music would stop." She and her co-organizer, Lindy Hernández, not only had to improvise constantly to ensure that the show would go on, but also had to keep that punk wildfire contained within the backyard, a task that did not always prove successful.

Whether it was a guy at the show going around with a knife and slashing tires on neighbors' parked cars all along Arboleda Drive or the city fining Oretgón's family $200 for a particularly loud show, the excitement did get out of control, but Ortegón could always rely on the punk community to have her back. When this fine really put the Arboleda House in jeopardy, for instance, her friend Fill Heimer did not leave her in the lurch. Heimer helped Ortegón write a letter to the city, successfully requesting an extension of the fine due date. Ortegón then organized another show to raise more funds and called on fellow punx, via her friend's zine, *Candy from Strangers*, to help pay the fine. In her plea, Ortegón invokes her friends' memories of "all the good times . . . WYNONA RIDERS, HICKEY, BRISTLE, zine distribution, shows, ALL the locals, the juice, the flat tires."[1]

The Arboleda House was a central point in an entire constellation of improvisation and collaboration during this second wave of Chuco punk. These shows reflected the do-it-yourself punk ethos. Scholar Michelle Habell-Pallán reminds us that these predominantly Mexican punx already had something similar rooted in their own traditions. She explains, "The do-it-yourself sensibility at the core of punk musical subcultures found resonance in the Chicana/o cultural practice of rascuache, or making do with limited resources."[2] From 1992 to 1997, punx furiously booked their own shows, created their own venues, made their own zines, and recorded their own sound—not from an entirely imported DIY punk ethos, but from a rascuache that was a practice and a feeling that imbued their words, songs, actions, and music with cultural pride and history. This feeling can also be seen in the increased presence of Chicanas like Ortegón and Hernández as local promoters accompanied the rise of pivotal Chicano promoters like Alex Martínez, Luis Mota, Erik Frescas, and Edmundo Valencia. All were pivotal in creating venues like the Rugburn and Lencho's Place.

While a rascuache ethos was the means to booking shows, selling merch, or building stages, pleasure and connection, not profit, were the goals of all this hard work. "It was fun," Ortegón explains. "It was like these bands started coming to play. You know people would come from all over town, so you'd meet new people. It was more like a community, the building of a community." This feeling of fun and community arose at a time when Chicago and New York were developing

Latinx punk scenes that unabashedly asserted their sense of pride and used punk rock to attack anti-Latinx racism in the punk scene and racist hostility throughout the United States. Indeed, the foundational role of Chuco hardcore bands like Sbitch and Revolución X in the rise of Latinx Hardcore punk rock revolution demonstrates how Chuco was key to this sonic revolution.

Not only was this second wave of Chuco punk more *Chicano*, then, but it was also more *chingona*[3] than before. Although women like Bobbie Welch and Gabriela Díaz illustrate the participation of women in the first wave of Chuco punk, the women in this second generation were involved in a wider variety of roles in the scene. Jenny Cisneros, Deana Montoya, Sara Reiser, and Laura Beard, among many others, were all in different punk bands at the time. Like other women in the scene, especially Chicanas, Ortegón and Hernández threw shows, but they also played in bands and created their own zines. Punx that identified as women were a pervasive force in second wave, making Chuco punk more chingona, and more punk rock than ever before.

Within the broader story of 1990s El Paso punk, this feeling of community fueled the ferocity and creativity of this generation of Chuco punx. By the time the Arboleda House was in full swing, this second generation had already matured into their own and begun to grow bolder, more confident, and more unified in their own sound and exploits. Lower Valley punx led the charge, closely followed by the West Side, as they remade and defied social, cultural, and geographic boundaries and borders in a frenzied pursuit to satiate their appetite for music and connection. Using national zines like *Book Your Own Fuckin' Life*, Chuco punx put their rascuache ethos to work as a flurry of new bands such as Los Paganos, Rope, the Sicteens, the Fall on Deaf Ears, the Frantiks, Second Hand Human, and At the Drive-In (ATDI) were formed and intensified their touring, broadening these punx' spatial reach. Moreover, Lower Valley and West Side punx began to overcome deeply entrenched class and ethnic divisions, all the while collaborating with punx in the Central and Northeast part of the city. They also transcended international boundaries as Edmundo Valencia and Erik Frescas solidified a transnational punk exchange in a time of increasing militarization of the border. At this time, punx were expanding the reach of Chuco along the border as well as nationally and even internationally, especially with ATDI landing their first major label deal and recording their debut album, *Acrobatic Tenement*.

The first hints of ATDI's rise are but one outburst in an entire cacophony of activity as these Chuco punx intensified their creative and geographic reach.

The first generation had passed the torch, and the second was poised now to set Chuco ablaze.

SEIZING THE SOUND OF THE CHUCOTOWN SOUNDTRACK

This new generation of punx was bursting with activity, and they immediately began to dominate Texas punk with copies of the fanzine *Book Your Own Fuckin' Life* in hand.

The fanzine became an indispensable tool in Chuco punx' hands. Just a quick look at the 1995 issue of *Book Your Own Fuckin' Life* sheds light on a Chuco scene that was teeming with creativity.[4] While just a year earlier, only one of the seventeen bands listed under "Texas" in *Book Your Own Fuckin' Life* were from El Paso,[5] by 1995, thirteen of the fifty-two Texas bands listed were from Chuco. (VBF has two ads, so there are actually fourteen Chuco ads.) The names of the bands provided include Bubble Gum Crisis, Gambini Beef Steak, the Fatsoz, Suicide Güeys, among a plethora of similarly rad band names. By comparison, in that same issue, nine Austin bands appeared, along with five from Houston and four from Dallas.[6] The year 1995 appears to be the apex of second wave Chuco punk, and in 1996, only eight out of fifty-three bands were from El Paso.[7] The center of punk gravity was definitely shifting Chuco-ward at this time, and El Paso record labels were pivotal to that wave.[8]

In 1993, out of the Lower Valley, Ernesto Ybarra created independent punk record label Yucky Bus, and his friends Carlos Palacios and Tony Leal created the Take That!!!! label. Ybarra and company had already reached out to the national punk community on tour with

VBF and brought home even more ways to grow the scene, like starting independent labels. He had made friends with Danny Buzzard and Devon Morph from the San Francisco punk band All You Can Eat. According to Ybarra, Buzzard and Morph were extremely influential in exposing Ybarra and others to DIY culture, which included starting up their own record label. These labels, especially Yucky Bus, were rascuache/DIY to the core, even at the level of recording. Ybarra's best friend Surge Mendoza became serious about recording bands, and he sharpened rascuache sound engineering to an art.

Mendoza and seven other family members lived in a house in the Lower Valley that had previously been a local site of coffin manufacturing. With this menacing mystique and Surge's engineering chops, his home became a key recording studio for punx. At age seventeen, he purchased a 4-track mixer and started doing sound for bands who came to town, which developed his engineering prowess and attracted the attention of punx who were eager to record and release their music with a more raw and less polished edge to their sound. Surge guided bands to his bedroom, where he placed his beloved 4-track mixer in the closet, and the bands played in the bedroom. Afterwards, the lead singer entered the closet to record the vocals. Fill Heimer reflects decades later that as a sound engineer, Surge brought something special to recording. Heimer explains, "You can record on the best equipment, but not capture the soul of the band. And somehow, Surge was always able to do that." With Surge's prowess, Yucky Bus became one of the city's staple independent labels.

Yucky Bus and Take That!!! were not the only games in town, though: the Western Breed label was also founded in 1993 by Arlo Klahr, and then handed to Jim Ward. Although both Western Breed and Yucky Bus were independent punk labels from the same city, the tone of the two labels could not be any more different. This contrast is most visible in the ways they promoted their labels in *Book Your Own Fuckin' Life*:

YUCKYBUS WRECKIDZ/GUIDO VASELINE
PRODUCTIONS

8321 Loma Terrace, El Pisshole, TX 79907. (915) 591-0040 (Urn)

We're a small DIY label from a town that sux! Our shitty punk rock releases are:

V.B.F. "MTV Kills 7", Shit/Potato Justice split 7", also we have Napolean comp 7" (Monkeybite) 4 sale!! Get all 3 4 $6 buxppd! Cummin' soon: Attempted Erns 7", Not Your Moms Comp 7", Motorheads Tribute 7".

Western Breed: WESTERN BREED RECORDS

PO Box 220291, El Paso, TX 79913- (915) 532-6113

A virtual plethora of independent punk rock/indie bands above description. Bands on vinyl are: Tu Edge, Crushstory, Out of Hand, Foss and At the Drive-In. Everyone tours, [buy] a record or two.[9]

The more serious tone of Western Breed contrasted with the irreverence of Yucky Bus. Ybarra explains that the piercing sense of humor was just part of growing up in the Lower Valley and coping with more serious problems. He notes, "It's like nonstop roasting each another, nonstop foolery, nonstop like *mamadas*. So it's kinda like, in a weird way, now that I think about it, I think it was because most of the time it was our way of coping with shit."

Western Breed was not entirely devoid of snark and humor. While Foss's *El Paso Pussycats* was their first release in 1993, the label's release of ATDI's first EP titled *Hell Paso* was a sardonic homage to their hometown. Although the profile of El Paso as a site of sound was increasing, Western Breed's release of *Hell Paso* and Yucky Bus's references to "El Pisshole," their hometown that "sux," all pay derisive homage to the city. Even in their disdain, Chuco permeates their consciousness, but also illustrates the diversity of labels flourishing in the city at the time, labels that were created through rascuache independence and fire.

Whatever their approach, these labels were emanating a Chuco sound right and left throughout the 1990s, which was a daunting task considering the vast range of sound emerging from the city at this time.

Sicteens' guitarist Abel Salazar describes the different genres of music coursing through Chuco at the time: grunge, death metal, hardcore and crust, pop punk, and emo. In a magazine interview decades later, Jim Ward's view is in line with Salazar's and points to a vast panorama of sound. For Ward, his hometown could not produce something as coherent as a DC or LA sound since musicians with punk, reggae, heavy metal, and a plethora of other backgrounds were all playing in bands in town. For him, the eclectic fusion brought something unique to the city's music.

> I've always thought the coolest thing about this city is that it's a free-for-all. I always describe this city as a frontier; it's called the Pass for a reason. People come and go and leave their imprints. . . . The identity's always been about total openness and collaboration.[10]

The hard work punx like Ybarra and Ward put into creating their record labels and advertising them in zines underline the rascuache ethos in practice during the second wave. Also, this generation of punx came of age at an opportune moment when *Book Your Own Fuckin' Life* fostered a Chuco connection to the vital national and international punk scenes. Creating things on their own was a quest in and of itself, but a sincere love of music and for one another was the dominant focal point and inspiration for second wave Chuco punk. In the early to mid '90s, it was this supportive free-for-all environment that encouraged unmoored creativity, openness, and collaboration. Labels like Yucky Bus, Take That!!!, and Western Breed had seized this dynamic sound, and now it was time to unleash it.

One of the major currents of sound was deeply political punk. Chuco hardcore in particular was not merely criticizing distant political hypocrisy and inequality. El Paso was ground zero in the implementation of historic social and economic policies in the '90s that took a devastating toll on the city. Chuco hardcore punk became a key flank in the broader sonic assault against the forces laying siege to their community.

THE RISE AND FALL OF ELOTE YOUTH: POLITICAL PUNK IN CHUCO

By the mid-1990s, dramatic national and international changes were playing out on a personal level for Chuco punx. Prior to 1994, Canadian, Mexican, and United States governments were working furiously to liberalize international trade markets. Bipartisan support for the North American Free Trade Agreement (NAFTA) secured its passage on January 1, 1994, and further soured many punx' taste for establishment politics. Naked Aggression lead singer Kirsten Patches describes how the menace of corporate globalization and the rise of neoliberalism (i.e., reform policies focused on market deregulation and the promotion of privatization)—most potently via the passage of NAFTA—were central to the punk politics of the era. She said, "Everything we had been yelling about in the '90s as a punk rock band, it started to become more of a blatant reality across the world as the '90s progressed."[11]

Chuco punx were already in the crosshairs of Patches' "blatant reality" of neoliberal globalization. The effects were devastating and swift, and within six months of NAFTA's passage, twenty-five garment plants in El Paso closed.[12] On November 3, 1997, Levi Strauss announced the closure of three El Paso plants that employed 1,500 workers, and Wrangler and Lee soon followed suit.[13] Between 1994 and 2001, 24,000 workers in the city lost their jobs due to NAFTA, making El Paso the American city with the largest number of NAFTA-displaced workers.[14] The effect on El Paso's garment workers, the majority of which were women, had ruinous impacts that struck this second generation of punx directly. Ernesto Ybarra's mother lost her job at Levi's, for example, and Eddie Martínez's mother's job at Levi's was relocated to San Antonio.

The community did not take these changes lightly. At the forefront of El Paso's resistance was an organization, La Mujer Obrera. Striking

Elote Youth flyer for a show with bands Pragmatic, Fall on Deaf Ears, Belvederes, Fla Fla Flunky, Suicide Güays, and the Ronias

Farah workers in the 1970s founded the institution that eventually became a resource center for garment and textile workers which provided advocacy around issues like education and housing. By the mid-1990s, founder Cecilia Rodríguez became the director of Centro del Obrero Fronterizo, and their central program service was La Mujer Obrera.[15] She was also the mother of prominent Central El Paso punk Kiko Rodríguez. This additional connection fueled the political strain of Chuco punk in the '90s.

When La Mujer Obrera collaborated with other labor groups to protest women workers losing their jobs at factories like Levi's in 1996, Kiko's punk band Second Hand Human, along with hardcore Lower Valley band Sbitch were eager to help. The two bands arranged a benefit show under the Bridge of the Americas in 1996 to raise money for the displaced workers. Kiko explains that benefit shows were important even if the bands did not entirely understand the gravity of the issues facing these workers. "We felt good about that day. We felt good about doing something with the scene that could help the local organization's push."

This opposition to NAFTA was part of a wider insurgence against globalization and the oppression of Indigenous and working peoples everywhere. The Ejército Zapatista de Liberación Nacional (EZLN), also known as the Zapatistas, is an Indigenous guerilla group in Chiapas, Mexico, which went public on the day NAFTA came into effect: January 1, 1994. It soon began what proved to be the most galvanizing of these rebellions. Motivated to get NAFTA passed through the Mexican congress, President Carlos Salinas de Gotari accelerated the liberalization of the Mexican economy, which undercut Indigenous rights to land and their ability to engage in self-sufficient farming. As a grassroots uprising with a non-hierarchical leadership structure, the Zapatista rebellion was especially compelling to Chuco punx for its ethnic composition and ideology, but also its style. If pachucos and punx used fashion as a tool, for the Zapatistas, it was a weapon. Comandante Marcos, the voice of the Zapatista rebellion, admitted, "We used facemasks because of the cold. But suddenly the facemasks caught on with the people, and so we kept them on."[16]

For Kiko, the fusion of labor and Zapatista politics found a natural medium of expression in his music and student activism. In addition to his mother's role with La Mujer Obrera, Cecilia Rodríguez also became the US representative for the EZLN, so her son's music could not go untouched by Zapatista politics. Kiko soon started a student activist group at Austin High School called Zapatista Youth. He promoted Zapatista politics at punk shows and had fundraisers for the Zapatistas, where Second Hand Human became known from others in the scene for selling *elote*. They then began to be known in the scene as Elote Youth, which Rodríguez was okay with because it helped to spread the message.

Despite the derisive nickname, in 1999, Comandante Marcos of the EZLN was very clear about the crucial role music played in the 1990s. Marcos emphasized how music was an essential "space of meeting" where, "the punks don't go around on a campaign demanding that all young people be punks, nor do the ska [kids], the goths, the metal [heads], the thrashers, the rappers, and certainly not the indigenous." For Marcos, their importance was rooted in how kids like Elote Youth were organizing a form of resistance, communicating politics just as Marcos and the EZLN were.[17]

Zapatista and anti-capitalist politics also inspired Gaspar Orozco, who was a college student at University of Texas at El Paso (UTEP) at the time. For years, Orozco had loved "the pure, brutal power" of punk rock and its inherent critique of social injustice. Inspired by the impending EZLN insurgency, he teamed up with his friend Antonio Martínez and formed hardcore punk band Revolución X. They recorded their self-titled debut EP on January 1, 1994, the day of EZLN's uprising.

The first track on the EP is a recording of Comandante Marcos reading the Zapatista manifesto. What follows in track two is pure rage in "E.Z.L.N.," a punk rock cacophony of support for the Zapatistas and a visceral critique of neoliberal and establishment Mexican politics.[18] Subsequently, Orozco sent out copies of the EP primarily to contacts through *Maximum Rocknroll* and released it with the support of four French punk labels: Ineptie, New Wave Records, Toxic Gravity, and

!Angrr!. The political and musical ferocity were the hooks, and the song "I'm Making My Future With the Border Patrol" is indicative of Revolución X's overall attack on hypocrisy and injustice along the border. In an eviscerating tone, Orozco opines of happily working for the border patrol and being the face of the land of the free, but suddenly submerges the listener in the nefarious reality:

> But if you want to get inside
> I'll kick out your teeth.
> I'm making my future with the border patrol.
> Beating Mexicans is so much fun![19]

The song is immortalized in the documentary *Beyond the Screams: Mas Allá de los Gritos: A U.S. Latino Hardcore Documentary*, where the lyrics are interspersed on the screen with shots of police officers in Riverside, California, mercilessly beating migrants along a highway in 1996.[20] The song obviously touches on broader injustices occurring in the '90s, both in California and closer to home.

Back home in El Paso, after years of litigation, the *Murillo v. Musegades* class action suit finally forced the Border Patrol to stop racially profiling Mexican Americans, which precipitated an overall reconfiguration of immigration enforcement tactics. The first step in this context was a change of leadership with El Paso native Silvestre Reyes assuming the role as Chief Patrol Agent of the El Paso Border Sector in 1993. Reyes revolutionized Border Patrol's strategy, changing it from one of pursuit to one of deterrence. This approach became known as "Operation Blockade" where the border became a fortress-like complex. San Diego immediately embraced Reyes' strategy under the name, "Operation Gatekeeper." As a result, it became impossible to cross illegally at specific ports of entry like El Paso and Tijuana.[21]

While the specter of the Border Patrol continued to loom over the border and inspire Revolución X's lyrics, Lower Valley hardcore band Sbitch focused on the impending environmental and cultural devastation that would result from neoliberal policies. Sbitch founder Alex

Martínez had already seen punk as an ideal form of political communication, in contrast to heavy political theory like that of influential anarchist, activist, and writer Emma Goldman. Martínez is frank: "I tried reading . . . Goldman, and I got bored to death. . . . I couldn't stomach anarchist theory, but . . . [We punx are] all about propaganda of the deed."

When Martínez met fourteen-year-old Bel Air High School student Jenny Cisneros at a show, he found the legendary voice of this seminal hardcore band Sbitch. Cisneros was a self-confessed weirdo who listened to a mix of female-fronted bands like Nausea, Bikini Kill, Antischism, and Siouxie and the Banshees. The female lead singers in these bands challenged gender norms while simultaneously delivering scathing political critique of the status quo. For Cisneros, an enduring ethics of "equality and peace" were key to the bands she listened to and to the sound and politics of Sbitch. On their 1998 split cassette with UK punk band P.U.S. released by Revolt Tapes and You're Not Normal Records, songs like "To The Earth," and "Stench of Greed" characterized the hardcore politics of this band. In the song "Pure Death," for example, Sbitch seizes upon humans' obsession with power and control that lays waste to the natural environment.

> Humanity has been so cruel
> Injected me with pain
> Earned my distrust in mankind
> I can never love again
> Upset the balance
> Leave me naked in the toxic rain
> Suffering (garbled??)
> my flesh singed with this pain
>
> Down will fall another
> Choking air will smother
> Kill our sisters and our brothers
> For the pleasure of the others[22]

Such environmentalism was but one thread in an overall Chuco punk response to the rise of neoliberal politics, deindustrialization, immigration politics, and Zapatista insurgency. With El Paso in the crosshairs of social, political, and economic upheaval of the '90s, Chuco hardcore punx exuded an especially relevant sonic critique and vitriol against injustice. They were not alone, but had key leaders Cecilia Rodríguez who rooted them in the everyday realities of those marginalized by supposedly liberating national and international policies.

But Chuco hardcore punk rock was also part of a broader revolution in punk. Punk rock was at a crucible, and punx of color were using the sound to reject racism both inside and outside the scene, and that reckoning came in the form of a Latinx punk insurrection.

NI DE AQUÍ, NI DE ALLÁ—LATINO PUNK INSURRECTION

Martín Sorrondeguy, lead singer of the band Los Crudos, restlessly paces like a caged lion in front of the jam-packed punk show in the Pilsen neighborhood of Chicago. The band and audience are silent as Sorrondeguy describes why he wrote the next song. He fumes:

> Some people in this music scene or whatever referred to Los Crudos as a "Spic band." Oh yeah, a "Spic band," but Martín's cool. Yeah that's what was said, "Oh yeah, Martín's a cool guy." No fuck you! I'm not a cool guy!

The largely Brown audience applauds, and Sorrondeguy scales up the intensity, so full of rage he practically spits out to the audience:

> Don't refer to me as a "Spic." . . . You are fucking part of the problem. Okay and it lets us know what we've been doing for so many years is right. And it's like I or anybody in this band who started this band and the kids from this neighborhood

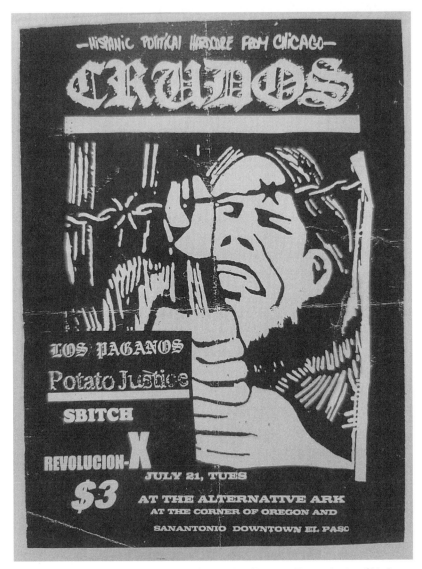

Flyer for a show in El Paso, featuring Los Crudos, Los Paganos, Potato Justice, Sbitch, and Revolución X

who have been coming to see us. None of us. None of us feel less than anybody else about where we were born; the language we speak; the foods we eat; what we're about; about our history; about our families. There's no shame, so things like that piss us off so bad.

His emotions come to a fever pitch. He's almost on the verge of tears as he addresses the Latinx punx in the crowd directly:

Está canción yo les dedico a toda la gente de este barrio y a todos nuestros amigos y compas.

He bends down towards his guitarist, as if conspiring to bring forth a smoldering flame. The first chords are struck. Sorrondeguy propels himself upwards, and lands as the crowd of punx propel themselves like a seething weather pattern. Sorrondeguy and the audience shriek to one another:

That's right motherfucker; we're that spic band!
You say you call yourselves punk?
BULLSHIT . . .
You just fucking fear us!
You're BULLSHIT!
That's right motherfucker; we're that spic band![23]

Chicago's Pilsen neighborhood was the site of this raucous sound, and it was also Los Crudos' home. (In 1990, 88 percent of Pilsen's residents were Latino, contributing to Cook County, Illinois, having the third largest Hispanic population in the US that year.)[24] Los Crudos were at the forefront of a broader movement, and the insurgent power of Chuco hardcore was intertwined with a nationwide renaissance of '90s Latinx hardcore punk rock. In a decade marked by increasing anti-Mexican immigration policies and racism, there was a hunger for pan-Latinx opposition to racism nationally and within the punk scene. Sorrondeguy explains, "The general xenophobia that was in the US. . . . It wasn't just a West Coast thing. All of a sudden there was a lot to sing about, a lot to write about, a lot to talk about."[25] This pent-up frustration and rage found expression in the most Latino of punk rock genres: hardcore punk rock. The first wave of punk rock, like that of Blondie and X-Ray Spex, eschewed the bombastic overtures of rock 'n' roll of the '60s and '70s and embraced a stripped-down sound that was infused with a touch of flair and artistic sensibility. By the 1980s, the subgenre of hardcore emerged with the likes of Bad Brains and TSOL. Hardcore punk's sound and pace raged at a much more intense pace with vitriolic political lyrics and disdain for the artistic flourishes of their forbearers in the late 1970s.

Indeed, there was a Latinx precedent at the roots of Hardcore punk: Boriqua Ron Reyes fronted the quintessential hardcore band Black Flag, and some critics like punk chronicler David Jones considered Alicia Armendariz "Alice Bag" Velasquez to be "the inventor of the West Coast hardcore punk sound."[26] Latinx hardcore was a key vehicle to express the struggles of Latinos in the US and an effective sonic weapon against anti-Latinx racism.

Although more than a thousand miles away, Los Crudos' confrontation with racism and their embrace of ethnic pride were tapping into issues deeply relevant to Chuco punx as well, especially the struggle for a sense of identity. The feeling of being "ni de aquí, ni de allá" is an enduring paradox embedded in Latinx/Chicanx identity: You don't belong to white society, but you have no substantive cultural connections to Mexico or the rest of Latin America. Chuco punk Sophia Orquiz explains, "I've struggled with identity most of my life. Not Mexican enough for some, not white enough for others." Lower Valley punk Jacob Trevizo goes into more detail about this broader identity crisis. "We're Mexican Americans. We're Chicanos. We speak more English than we do Spanish, and that's a colonial language anyways. You have all these layers of who we are, who they say we are. . . . We don't really fit in. We're not Mexican enough for the Mexicans because they call me '*pocho*.'"

Many Chuco punx also had to grapple with the rigid and highly racialized images of Mexican culture and punk culture. In 1997, Erica Ortegón described in her friend's zine, *Candy From Strangers*, how she had failed a magazine quiz titled "Are Your Pura Latina?" According to the quiz, she was a "pseudo Latina" because she was too assimilated. She explained, "Just because I wear Converse tennis shoes instead of high heels, they say I deny my Latina blood. Also, because I didn't know who Selena was until she died means I'm not Latina?"[27] Caught between rigid perceptions of Mexican identity and the white racialization of punk rock, Chicana punx like Ortegón had little room to maneuver. As late as 1998, a retired *Profane Existence* coeditor simply listed as "joel" wrote a column titled "ABOLISH THE WHITE PUNK," in which he takes aim at anti-Black racism in the scene but continues to assert that most punks were middle class, educated, and white. Joel becomes exasperated and dismissive when he notes that there are even "Mexican and/or Chicanx punk scenes in several cities," which only serves to reinforce that white image of punk that he is criticizing.[28] In both mainstream and underground media, superficial understandings of the complexity of Latino identity emerge. The *Profane Existence* article illustrates what Habell-Pallán identifies as "the long held assumptions that unconsciously erase the influence of Latinos from popular music's sonic equation."[29]

Even in a predominantly Mexican and Indigenous city like El Paso, there was a pervasive silence around Chicanx identity and history. Coronado High School student and West Side punk Martha Yvette Martínez, for example, graduated at the top of her class, but still "felt very let down by educators at the time" due to the lack of Chicanx history and culture being taught in El Paso. The educational experiences were not only about silence, but outright whitewashing of history and identity. Sicteens drummer Tony Leal and his cousin, Sicteens guitarist Eddie Martínez, for instance, were encouraged to not speak Spanish in elementary school and to embrace the anglicized names "Tony" and "Eddie" instead of their real names, Luis Antonio and Edmundo Estevan. Kiko Rodríguez tells of his experience having to sing a Disney song about Davy Crockett, thereby honoring the namesake of his middle school. In retrospect, Rodríguez acknowledges that the school's reasons for having them sing the song might have been innocent, but, he says, "It was a bunch of Brown kids singing about how Davy

Crockett was our hero, and that was the environment in Texas because in the Texas educational books, there was no mention of Mexico at all, especially back then. There was no mention of the Mexican-American War. It was just, Mexicans didn't exist. It was so bizarre singing about a guy who slaughtered my people, both native and Mexican."

The accumulation of racist experiences found expression in the ethnic pride espoused by Latinx hardcore bands who sang in Spanish. Chuco punx like Kiko soon followed suit, and his band Second Hand Human began to use quotes from Subcomandante Marcos in songs such as "We're Watching You," and they often sang their songs entirely in Spanish.

Revolución X were also part of this Latinx punk revolution. First, Sorrondeguy's independent label Lengua Armada put out Revolución X's second EP in 1995 titled *Política y Esparcimiento*. The role Revolución X played in the movement superseded musical and personal connections; the ties were deeply rooted in a ferocious assault on racism in the 1990s. The entire EP was sung in Spanish, and their song "Corrido de Pete Wilson Y la 87" harnessed the rebellious history of *corridos* to critique Proposition 187. In 1994, voters in California overwhelmingly approved Proposition 187, which banned all public services to undocumented immigrants, the majority of whom were Mexican. California's governor at the time, Pete Wilson, was Proposition 187's most ardent supporter, and, hence, Revolución X's central target in the ballad.

Entre sus nuevas propuestas	Among their new proposals
Trae la 187	187 is brought out
Que pa'l indocumentado	So that for the undocumented
Sólo significa muerte	It only means death.
Sin escuelas ni hospitales	Without schools nor hospitals,
Se nos pretende dejar,	They aim to leave us.
Y aunque duro trabajamos	And although we work hard,
Se nos quiere eliminar	They want to get rid of us.

Vamos a luchar, hermanos	We are going to fight, brothers
En la Unión Americana	In the United States
Y que a Wilson y a su gente	So that Wilson and his people
Se los lleve a la chingada	Go to hell.[30]

Orozco was deeply historical and precise in his choice of a corrido as the vehicle for his message. He reflects how after Mexico lost 55 percent of its territory in 1848 after the Mexican-American War, corridos were key forms of sonic resistance against anti-Mexican racism in these now "occupied territories." According to Orozco, "The corridos were very important in the Mexican revolution, and it has been a quite practical way to tell stories. And in that way, it's a natural tool to establish instances of resistance, and I think that happened along the border and in the occupied territories. I thought that in the case of Pete Wilson and the Proposition 187 that a corrido was a good way to express what we thought about that, no?" Like "Contrabando de El Paso" and "El Corrido de Juana Gallo," the subversive nature of the corrido also informed Revolución X's sound. Orozco's use of a deeply Mexican genre reinforces the Mexican/Latinx pride that fueled the broader Latinx Hardcore punk revolution.

Revolución X was the quintessence of Latinx hardcore punk rock, and their fellow Chuco punx in Second Hand Human and Sbitch were integral to this revolution in multiple ways. Their sound was intertwined with the movement, and they were friends and collaborators with Los Crudos. Both Sbitch and Revolución X feature in the film Sorrondeguy made in the '90s, *Beyond the Screams: Mas Allá de los Gritos: A U.S. Latino Hardcore Documentary*. Chuco punx also had a deep well of experiences to fuel this Latinx Hardcore fire, especially the pressure to assimilate into white American culture, even though they weren't fully accepted in that culture, or Latin American culture, or the wider punk culture.

This political tenor was felt throughout the country as Brown punx started finding their voices, sound, and politics. While attacking Proposition 187 or asserting their ethnic pride, Chuco punk politics was sonically unfettered, uncontrollable, shattering borders in its wake, and part of a formidable movement of Latinx punx in the '90s.

But Chuco punk could also be dorky, *chistoso*, full of *mamadas*, and cheesy as hell.

"CHEESY ASS PUNK ROCK": ROCKIN' FOR THE HELL OF IT IN CHUCO

Lower Valley hardcore band VBF were political like their friends in Los Crudos and Sbitch, but they also excelled at not taking themselves too seriously. They were blunt when describing themselves in *Book Your Own Fuckin' Life*: "Voted the worst band in the South! Three dorks deliver cheesy ass punk rock str8 out of Compton!!"[31]

VBF were definitely not alone with this irreverence, and their successors, The Sicteens, took this audacious fun to another level. Carlos Palacios was the mastermind of the zany band and was very intentional about finding the right people for the undertaking. Thankfully, Palacios became quick friends with Tony Leal, a fellow Samhain fan. This love of all things Misfits made the arrival of Leal's fellow Bel Air High School Misfits crew a natural fit in what coalesced into the Chuco punk mainstays: the Sicteens.

Although they were all Glen Danzig devotees, the Sicteens unabashedly embraced a "fun loving Ramones style punk."[32] Their style was the first tip-off: the four guys donned leather jackets and sunglasses like their punk idols. They even had a band mascot, "Rocky Ramone." Friend Rob Harrington created a Joey Ramone-esque character, and even a mythology of the band and the mascot. In a comic strip Harrington drew for a Sicteens EP, Rocky's own leather jacket disintegrates after traveling through time. However, The Sicteens appear in front of Rocky and present him with a new leather jacket and christen him "The Sicteen."

The band's sound was fun-loving pop punk. In their song, "A.P.B.," for example, Palacios pines for his girlfriend who went to the laundromat, but had to put an APB on her because, "She said she'd be right back / I don't know where she is / I don't know where she's at."

Beginnings of the Sicteens. Pictured are Tony Leal and Carlos Palacios.

When Palacios needed three video samples to get into art school, he used the opportunity to make a music video for "A.P.B." The lo-fi video follows the guys in The Sicteens driving through the city in a Ford Bronco. At one point, guitarist Eddie Martínez bursts out of a porta potty, mocking Slash's melodramatic guitar solo in the music video for "November Rain." It was a good-humored punk take down of the bombast represented by Guns n' Roses and other bloated, self-important hair bands of the day.

Despite the video being just an assignment, it played on the televisions throughout Ysleta High School that were used to broadcast the "Channel One" news program. The video even played on El Paso's public access channel. The members of the band never saw it televised, but Leal and Martínez's four-year-old cousin, Julian, called Leal every time he saw the video on public access and shouted, "Tony, I saw your stupid video on TV, again, and it sucks!"

The ties of humor and fun that are still apparent in these relationships were also infused into the band Fixed Idea's sound. Take the song "Chucotown Ska" for instance:

Just wanna dance with my baby tonight.
Because the bass is thumping everybody's pumping to the
heavy, heavy sounds of the heavy heavy Chucotown ska
Don't give a shit about animal rights
I'm gonna party on the hilltop tonight.[33]

The Chucotown soundtrack encompassed a range of sounds. From hardcore soliloquies about death to putting out an APB for your girl-friend, Chuco punk was rife with creativity and diversity. What also united them was a maturing sense of community and a devotion to the rascuache ethos that fueled this frenzy of activity, impelling them to roam across the city and the border to satiate their appetite for live music.

SEIZING THE SPACE: SHOWS IN CHUCOTOWN

Fixed Idea, Crawl Space, Stressed Out, and Degreen were set to play a backyard show at a friend's house in the spring of 1993. The turnout was expected to be especially big because they had kegs of beer to fur-ther entice local punx with an insatiable appetite for punk rock, fun, and cheap alcohol. The flyers also alerted the El Paso Police Depart-ment, and when Lower Valley punk Fill Heimer and other organizers found out that the cops were poised to bust the show, they innovated.

As punx paid the cover and filed into the backyard, the organiz-ers marked their hands and told them to meet at a local Peter Piper Pizza once the police raided the show, and to wait for further direc-tions. The night started with Heimer's band Crawl Space taking the stage armed with their Minor Threat and Fugazi covers. An El Paso Police Department helicopter started to circle the show, and a spot-light fell on Heimer as he belted out "Waiting Room." "I felt like a badass," says Heimer. The masses of punx immediately fled from the police and descended upon the local pizza joint, where a strategically placed punk directed them to a nearby reservoir named "the Cave." There, the bands, a generator, and the precious kegs awaited them.

Even without a backyard, Chuco punx made do with just music, a generator, and beer.

From 1993 to 1997, shows like this reveal how Chuco punx propelled the evolution of live music innovation forward in the face of daunting odds. Their fully honed rascuache skills becomes apparent as punx scoured the city for anything from discarded rugs to extra lumber to create viable venues for punk bands. They played anywhere, from the desert to back alleys. This synergy gave this second generation, especially Chicana punx, the opportunity to cut their teeth on setting up shows, poising them to become key promoters years later.

While Chuco punx continued to utilize the standard venues like school cafeterias, backyards, and venues like the Attic, the Custom Queen, Club 101, the Golden Age Center, and the Mesa Inn, their approach became more refined, sophisticated, and strategic, and their reach broader in scope. Erica Ortegón's Arboleda House was one of the most notable, but it wasn't the sole backyard emitting punk sound for this second generation. Surge Mendoza, Carlos Palacios, Verna López, and Erik Frescas are but a handful of the masses of Chuco punx that were reconfiguring their ordinary backyards into vibrant sites of live music and connection. The success of these shows, however, also made them a target for the El Paso Police Department.

Erik Frescas recounts one show that started in his own backyard. His mom begrudgingly acquiesced to the show but told Frescas that he was on his own if the cops showed up, which they did. Even before the first band started playing to a crowd of around two hundred punx, the arrival of the cops had the punx jumping the backyard gate, fleeing from the EPPD. According to Frescas, once the SWAT team arrived, "All chaos breaks loose," and the punx eventually moved the show two or three times. By the end of the night, there were only about twenty people left listening to the bands play between an apartment complex and a basketball court.

Punx enjoyed the explosive energy of shows in backyards and house shows throughout El Paso and the entire Tri-Cities Area, made up of El Paso, Juárez, and Las Cruces, New Mexico. West Side punk Peter Friesen remembers one ATDI show he saw in Las Cruces where

the band was playing inside the house, with a sliding glass door separating the band from the audience out in the backyard. While lighting
a Christmas tree on fire at the show was fun, what was most memo-
rable was ATDI's performance. Friesen remembers, "And it was really
cool because Cedric [Bixler-Závala] started using the door as part of
a way to change his singing. He was opening and shutting the glass
door, which was causing it to be loud and then muted and loud and
muted. It was pretty intense."

Despite how dynamic ATDI shows were, ATDI's own experiences
playing shows in Chuco left them baffled. In published interviews
decades later, both Bixler- Závala and Ward expressed their frustration with the lack of local support for ATDI. While the band played
to large crowds outside of El Paso, when they returned home, they
played to "nobody a lot of times."[34] This experience was not isolated.
Lindy Hernández's first issue of her *Candy From Strangers* zine in
1996, for example, reveals even more powerfully how widespread this
problem really was. In her column titled "Frustration," she talks about
how excited she was to go to new punk venue the Rugburn and "listen to the musik we like the most," but she was pissed because punx
weren't going inside for the show. Instead, they were found outside the
show, bumming cigarettes and beer. Hernández explained:

> That's not what shows are about. People should support the
> bands, they've fucken worked hard to go on tour and deserve
> an appreciative audience. So if you really want to support the
> scene. Get your ass in there, Support the bands & Buy your
> beer LATER![35]

The explosion of backyard shows, desert shows, and even shows
in alleys infused boring and static geographic sites of El Paso with
the rollicking Chuco. The fun and innovation had its limits, though.
Police busting backyard shows and cheap punx bumming 40s in the
parking lot instead of supporting the bands were consistent problems
in this scene.

Despite the frustration, Chuco punx continued to innovate and collaborate, eventually creating important music venues instead of bouncing around backyards.

They were creating the Rugburn!

MOST DEFINITELY A RIOT: THE RUGBURN RIOT OF '96

By 1996, Lower Valley punx Alex Martínez and Carlos Palacios were increasingly frustrated with these instances of police busting backyard shows. They had also inherited a ton of amps and speakers that were proving way too heavy to lug around town. They needed a place like The Rugburn.

First, they had the guys from the Fla Fla Flunkies put up the money to rent a car repair shop that was located on the main strip of Alameda Ave. Their choice was strategic because the venue was right off a major exit on I-10, making it easily accessible to punx throughout the city. They then put their rascuache ethos to work by soundproofing the small venue. They covered it with carpet and rugs, and they nailed upholstery sponge to the ceiling. The prevalence of rugs everywhere inspired its name: the Rugburn.

There were already venues like Club 101 and the Attic in town, but The Rugburn was going to be something different. Really, Martínez and Palacios wanted the Rugburn to be a non-profit music venue along the lines of Berkeley's 924 Gilman Street, a place that brought in out-of-town bands and sidestepped for-profit music ventures. Additionally, the Rugburn was created to overcome regional rivalries—especially between the West Side and the Lower Valley—and become a place where all punx could come to watch live music together.

The Rugburn was a deeply rascuache venture focused on community, not profit, so a manifesto was necessary to articulate these aims. In the manifesto, titled "Our Cause," they were adamant that the Rugburn would be a place where they would be "united as a strong scene." At the Rugburn, they had a place "to look beyond each other's skin color, ethnic background, and sex to just have a good time and know that we are there for a common cause." To underline the importance of solidarity in the scene, the author includes the lyrics of the Los Crudos song, "Unidad Prohibida"—"Forbidden Unity":

And I don't care what color you are,
Where you're from,
If you're Guatemalan, Mexican, Nicaraguan, Salvadorean, Honduran, Puerto Ricans, Cuban, Panamanian, Dominican, Columbian, Venezuelan, Ecuatorian [sic], Peruvian, Bolivian, Brazilian, Chilean, Paraguayan, Argentine, Uruguayan, North American, Asian, African, or European
There's no excuse
We're In this together.[36]

The manifesto illustrates how thoughtful and strategic Chuco punx were in their quest for community. Their choices were often-times very intentional and politically informed, like at the Rugburn. The use of a Los Crudos song in their manifesto further solidifies Chuco punk within the broader Latinx punk movement. The shared ideals of pan-Latinx identity expressed in "Unidad Prohibida" sheds light on the underlying shared ethos of Latinx Hardcore punk: racial unity, especially Latinx unity that transcends nationality.

These earnest goals of facilitating connection and community had to be accomplished by the practical and hard work of booking bands and keeping the peace with neighbors. The Rugburn started booking local bands like Debaser and Sbitch and out-of-town bands like Anti-Flag and The Peeps. This was not an easy undertaking, how-ever. In a Rugburn Announcement titled "Over 100 El Paso Punks Can't Be Wrong... The Rugburn Rocks!!" the venue's promoters, Alex Martínez, Lindy Hernández, Erik Frescas, and Ernie Rivera, note that even though the Rugburn was created to be "El Paso's Only Punk-Rock-Hardcore, All-Ages Hangout/Community Center," the rest of the scene was slacking in the everyday efforts of keeping the venue afloat. They explained, "Some of us are sick of begging bands and making flyers." Since there were no owners, "just shit workers," they called on the scene to play their part.[37]

They were not exaggerating.

Booking shows and keeping the peace with neighbors were daunting tasks. Once they started the shows, they soon realized that the building was not only shared with another business, but a family lived in that building and had access to the breaker box. When shows became too loud, they cut off the electricity abruptly. Eventually, Martínez and Palacios were able to smooth things over with the owner of the building and with the family, who soon began to send their son down to sell sodas, *cacahuates*, *dulces*, and *chicles* during the shows.

Although created to be a safe site of sound, cramming feisty and sweaty punx into a small car repair shop was bound to ignite some mayhem . . . like the Rugburn Riot of November 1996.

According to Martínez, they had booked a "pulverizing metal hardcore" show made up of bands like San Francisco's Strychnine and Albuquerque's Word Salad. There was an intensity in the air, and Jessica Flores decided to leave early because, "You could feel it. You could definitely feel it. Something was going to happen." When talking to one of the guys from Strychnine before the show, West Side punk Luis Mota remembers asking the guys about the craziest show they had ever played. The guy from Strychnine responded forebodingly, "We were playing this show in Europe, and a riot broke out."

The underlying unease fused with a packed show and an array of punk gangs. Some of the gangs included SHARPs, cholo punx, the Animal Liberation Front, and the Plant Liberation Front, making the mix of punx all the more combustible. There are conflicting views on the cause. Some say it was a fight in the pit; others claim a cholo punk had brandished a pistol. What everybody agrees on, however, was that one of Martínez's friends decided to call the police. Martínez responded, "Why did you call the police? That's going to make it worse!"

Five to six police cars immediately surrounded The Rugburn. According to Martínez, some West Side punx parked across the street and jumped into their truck to leave, and a police officer pulled out his gun and made the punx get out of the truck, then started kicking one of them in the head. Martínez shouted at the police officer to stop and called out the badge number of the cop who kicked his friend. When Martínez kept shouting "Nobody move!" to other punx, a cop came right for him. The cop took hold of him, but Martínez was able to get free of his grip and start running. Then, according to Martínez:

> The cops got ahold of me and started beating me up on the car, pounding my head into the hood of Jason's [Cagann] car, and then, out of nowhere, I see Ernie [Rivera], and [the cops] are both punching us in the face and in the head. And Jenny [Cisneros] told me that when they were doing that, they were holding the crowd away with their shotguns pointed at the crowd.

Jason Cagann remembers police assaulting Martínez and slamming him down on the hood of his car. He and his friends were trying to make the police stop, but the police formed a barrier between the group of friends and Martínez. Cagann remembers:

> They wouldn't even turn around; they were looking at us. We were like, "Your buddies are beating up our friend! Just turn around! Look!" And they wouldn't. And then this male officer got a shotgun and pointed [it] at us, and we had our hands up. . . . It was very scary because he was not comfortable. He was very fidgety. He looked really nervous. It was strange because we were like, . . . "It's just us dumbasses!"

Luis Mota, who says he was standing by his friend's car, "waiting till all this shit [died] down," was approached by a police officer, and the officer put a shotgun right into his face and ordered him to freeze. Mota remembers how "it got way more out of hand than it should have." West Sider Peter Friesen remembers a similarly chaotic scene "with people running everywhere." Once he was outside the Rugburn, a police officer ordered him to get in his car. When Friesen did get into his car to leave, the officer berated him for not leaving even though the officer's car was parked right behind Friesen, preventing him from going anywhere.

While shows did occur after the Rugburn Riot, it was as if the riot were the dramatic crescendo of this punk venue. The lingering issues of getting punx involved and making money from the shows soon came to a head at the end of 1996, and the venue closed.

In all its fury and brevity, the Rugburn was the quintessence of rascuache. It wasn't just the use of discarded lumber and rugs to build the venue. It was the push to create a site of sound that was focused on inclusivity and unity rather than profit, especially between the Lower Valley and the West Side.

But the Rugburn's purpose ran up against the reality of only a handful of punx doing all the work, instead of the responsibility being shared throughout the community they sought to unite. The venue and community also confronted the reality of law enforcement's willingness to brutally squash their fun.

Despite the Rugburn's short-lived existence, Martínez is proud that it was "a culmination of the kids from all the scenes coming together, all the different parts of town, and also in Juárez." Martínez also acknowledges that the Rugburn was only one of many sites of sound. The other was a punk rock bridge with their homies in Juárez that punx were furiously building and traversing.

"LENCHO'S PLACE"

Police surveillance and brutality created barriers for movement and sound, but so too did the international border between El Paso and Juárez. Despite the deepening divide between these intimately tied cities, Edmundo "Mundo" Valencia, a punk living in both Juárez and El Paso, and Chuco punk Erik Frescas, solidified an international connection between the two scenes. Mundo describes how zines like *Maximum Rocknroll* and *Profane Existence* inspired him to engage in such an endeavor.

By 1995, Valencia had tapped into a rich vein of punk. Bands like

Punk Edmundo "Mundo" Valencia in front of Lencho's Place in Ciudad Juárez

72 Horas, Los Beats, La Perdición, among many others were raging at the time. According to punk journalist Christina Oaxaca, it was also "the dawn of the *jilotepunks* (punks from Jilotepec, a neighborhood in the southeast of the city)." This vibrant scene had key venues like Teatro de la Asegurada where the shows became so intense that afterwards, the venue was littered with "pyrotechnics, sweat and blood on the stage," but something was missing, and that was a connection to punx across the river.[38]

This desire to forge a truly international live scene found expression when Mundo met Frescas outside a bar called La Raya in Juárez in 1996. Frescas was handing out flyers for a show, and the subsequent conversation with Mundo culminated in nascent plans to book bands to play shows both in El Paso and in Juárez. Frescas was keen to collaborate with Mundo because he knew the power of Mexican audiences. He reflects how bands in El Paso were always "hoping for that Mexico crowd" since they were known to arrive without notice in busloads delivering a charged presence to any live show.

One of the first steps in attracting touring bands to Juárez was to advertise in *Book Your Own Fuckin' Life*. When bands responded to the following ad, Frescas offered the bands to play only one show in El Paso and another in Juárez the following night. His 1996 ad read:

Will be able to hook-up bands with a place to play from clubs to back yards. I will try to provide food and or lodging.[39]

It was difficult for bands to play in Juárez because, upon returning to the States, they would have to show receipts for the purchase of their equipment to Mexican Customs officials. If they could not produce those receipts, their equipment would be considered an import, and they would have to pay an importation fee. Therefore, Mundo took the next step of booking Juárez bands "under the premise that they would have to share their equipment" with the visiting bands. Once they gained momentum, Mundo and Frescas booked a host of El Paso bands like Los Perdidos, the Hellcats, Fla Fla Flunkies, Debaser, Sbitch, and touring bands like Hickey to play in El Paso and later in Juárez at a venue called "Lencho's Place."

Named after the San Lorenzo neighborhood of Juárez where it was located ("Lencho" is the nickname for Lorenzo), the venue was a repurposed commercial space in front of the home of Hector "Winkle" Meraz. It had a garage that was detached from the house, and once Winkle and Valencia started Los Paganos, Winkle agreed to have El Paso bands play in the garage, and Lencho's Place became a hot punk venue.

It is important to note that this was largely a Lower Valley/Juárez endeavor. When podcaster Damien Abraham asked Cedric Bixler-Závala in 2018 if there was "any interaction with the punk stuff happening in Juárez," West Sider Bixler-Závala said no. While he acknowledged that there were shows going on in the late '90s in Juárez, he added, "It wasn't territory we would go do. We didn't know how to do that."[40] ATDI was actually booked to play an El Paso and then a Juárez show in 1996, along with Hickey and Los Perdidos. Valencia explains that when his band Los Paganos arrived at The Attic in El Paso to play with ATDI, he wasn't even sure who ATDI was, but "there was some problem or confusion, and the venue double booked the date," so ATDI did not play Lencho's Place.

Although there were occasional missed opportunities, Chuco punx were tenacious in their pursuit of live music despite the presence of an international border and a lack of all-ages venues. Their thinking about live music was informed, thoughtful, passionate, but also expansive. These punx disregarded established political boundaries, and forged a Chuco that was more all-embracing, one that truly incorporated El Paso, Juárez, and Las Cruces. In more ways than one, these punx recreated a Chuco more aligned with scholar Saldaña-Portillo's "one cultural landscape."[41] They did it not only for sound, but for fun and friendship, and a growing sense of ethnic pride that was growing in the '90s.

All this activity was in pursuit of a tenuous sense of belonging that they could not find elsewhere.

KICKFLIPS & CHORDS AT THE EDGELANDS AND OUTSKIRTS

Morehead Middle School in El Paso is auspiciously located on Confetti Drive—a celebratory name for an awesome skating experience that West Side punx Martha Yvette Martínez and Luis Mota seized regularly.

Really, it was Morehead's roof that was the draw for these punx' insatiable appetites for danger. There was a sidewalk near the entrance of the school where they could easily jump onto the roof. What lay before them on the roof was not a flat surface, but was like a mini-mountain range with many peaks, ideal for an awesome skate session. Martínez describes the scene via text:

> The peaks were small enough (no bigger than three feet) for
> us to gain some momentum to execute an ollie or kickflip
> from them. The thought of sneaking onto such an accessible
> but forbidden place was half of the thrill. I imagined the roof
> like a heart monitor _/\/\/_ carefully measuring our excited
> hearts. It was liberating!

Chuco skaters really left no space untouched, but the experience was different for girls and queer kids. Skateboarder and scholar Dani Abulhawa sees skateboarding as a way for skaters to "demonstrate a physical and creative rewriting of the urban environment," but Abulhawa would see them occupying "an edgeland position in [skateboarding] subculture." This edgeland position arises from female skateboarders being seen as an aberration, an assumption rooted in the "perception of skateboarding as being male dominated, potentially injurious, and physically aggressive." Despite being resigned to these edgelands, Abulhawa observes that female skateboarders transgress these perceptions, just as Martínez and Mota trespassed onto Morehead Middle School property.[42]

The imposition of a view of punk rock as white, male, heterosexual, and middle class is similar to that of skateboarding. Hence, when we look at the roles women, queer kids, and Black punx played in Chuco punk, we are seeing punx residing at similar edgelands, but ones with the potential to be trespassed. In Chuco punk, there were openings for liberation, but there were also limits embedded in the scene. Forms of expression that challenged such barriers were integral to the music culture.

This complexity can best be seen with punx' love of live music. For so many, sharing live music fostered a feeling of belonging that could not be accessed anywhere else. Fill Heimer emphasizes the profound emotional coalescence and transcendence that live music ignited for him. Shows, for Heimer, were "definitely a spiritual experience, sharing something together and becoming part of the bigger crowd." Abel Salazar from The Sicteens went one step further and admitted that the community he found at shows was a family that he didn't have at home. For Sbitch lead singer Jenny Cisneros, shows were so inspiring because "it's [a] community of people out there in the world who give a shit about something and want to have fun doing it." Live music provided a transcendent coalescence of fun, belonging, and passion.

Despite the alternative sound space that provided freedom for this punk community, the feeling of acceptance and inclusion was not always felt by all women or queer punx in the scene. The mix of accessibility and limitations of punk space is a widespread issue. Black culture critic and poet Hanif Abdurraqib challenges the supposed "brotherhood of punk" rooted in ideals of rebelliousness and inclusivity. He raises the crucial issue of "who sits at the outskirts or who sits at the bottom while the brotherhood dances oblivious and heavy at the top." For him, people of color, women, and the queer community are these intimate outsiders in the scene.[43] Although the Chuco scene was predominantly punx of color and much more open than other spaces to women's full participation, there was a complex mix of accessibility for queer folks. (Also, though they certainly participated, I was unfortunately unable to speak with any Black punx about their perspectives on the scene.)

Women often occupied this edgelands or outskirts existence in punk culture. Some of the punx pushing up against such exile were prominent punx Leah Lloyd, Sara Reiser, and Laura Beard. Lloyd explains that music was the foundation of the three girls' friendship, and that bonding inspired them to start the band the Glitter Girls. Later, Reiser and Beard became a formidable team on their own in their new band, Rope.

With the frenzy and energy of Bratmobile and scathing humor presaging the cutting social critique of Huggy Bear, Rope fed the '90s demand for authenticity and an unapologetic embrace of women's experiences. Subverting social discomfort with women's bodies, Rope's track "Menstrual Cramps" is a fast-paced and concise punk discussion of teenage girls and their periods. (This is definitely the antecedent of TacoCat's "Crimson Wave.")

"Leave Me Alone," on the other hand, speaks to the lack of public space and safety afforded to women.

> Why don't you just leave me alone!?
> Can't you see I don't want you here!?
> I have to leave, and it's all because of you.[44]

Revulsion over women's bodies and women's safety in public are '90s themes most commonly tied to the rise of the Riot Grrrl movement. However, a spectrum of feminist bands flourished in the 1990s. Bikini Kill, Bratmobile, and Sleater-Kinney are the standard bearers of Riot Grrrl, but other punk bands like Spitboy and more heavy metal bands like L7 were avowedly feminist, but not necessarily Riot Grrrl. Although there were significant differences, they were all responding to the same socio-historical context as Rope. One of the first and foremost historical markers of this period was the 1991 Senate Judiciary Committee's dismissive treatment of Law Professor Anita Hill

Laura Beard playing a gig in her band Rope

and her allegations of sexual harassment against then-Supreme Court nominee Clarence Thomas. The disregard for Hill's experience was matched only by the pervasive trivialization of feminism in popular media. The sound of this supposed death-knell for feminism is most vivid in *Time* magazine's 1998 cover: "Is Feminism Dead?" Music could not go untouched by such dismal proclamations, either. The rape and murder of the Gits lead singer Mia Zapata in 1993 reinforced that even in punk/alternative music scenes and public spaces, women's safety was tenuous. Music, in particular punk music, became a potent force of challenging sexist violence in the 1990s and further upended any misconceptions that feminism was an embarrassing vestige of the past. Therefore, bands like Rope embraced a sound and message that reflected these social, cultural, and historical currents. Chuco punk contributed to this overall movement just as much as other, more noted scenes like Olympia or DC.

Leah Lloyd, Sara Reiser, and Laura Beard also found a platform to express their views in the vibrant punk culture of zine-making. A photo of Susan B. Anthony appears on the cover of one issue with the vertically collaged *Femme Fatale* cascading along the right margin of this explicitly feminist zine. The three zine writers, along with their fellow punk contributors, take a focused attack on misogyny and sexism. Reiser, for example, moves from the personal to the historical in a typed zine column.

> Some people say that the oppression of women no longer exists, but it does. As women, we are given so many standards and so many "ideals" to live by. Of course, it is our decision whether we fit the description, or whether we will decide to be who we are, freely discarding what is expected, what can often be overwhelming and tiresome. . . . The speaking out of women began many years ago, and it has always been looked down on as a bad thing. As man-hating, and as jealously towards men. Which is definitely not the objective, or even the thoughts of feminists."[45]

Beard's handwritten, cursive-laden critique on the absence of women in bands also includes empowering steps to address the problem.

> I have yet to see any girl bands in El Paso. However, at shows . . . I see crowds of girls who really seem to be enjoying the music . . . and with such interest, I can't understand why those girls don't get out there and play music. When it comes to playing an instrument all it takes is little dedication and willingness, and I'm sure that there are a lot of girls with killer voices yet all the talent is hidden somewhere in the crowd. I hope to encourage you girls to get out there and get practicing. I'd be more than willing to help you girls out with equipment or anything else. . . . Let's not be the majority in the crowds and the minority when it comes to playing music.

Lloyd, Reiser, and Beard also pulled in the ranks of male allies to contribute to the zine. Alex Martínez, for example, targeted gender

Sara Reiser playing a gig in her band Rope

inequality with an article on "M.A.N. (Military Affairs Neurotic)," and New Wave Distro that Martínez, Palacios, and Frescas ran also advertised in the zine.[46]

Despite the support of their friends, when *Femme Fatale* was released, according to bandmate Clint Newsom, many people slandered the zine. But from his perspective, Reiser and Beard thrived on the opposition, making them work harder, and causing others in the scene to challenge their own conceptions of gender roles.[47] What is clear here is that while Beard and Reiser confronted the limits gender posed in Chuco punk, it was the same punk rock culture, via music, zines, and punk community, that allowed them to find expression for their critiques.

As a promoter and musician, Lindy Hernández also found her voice with her zine *Candy From Strangers*. First started around late 1996, the zine encapsulated the musings and currents of Chuco punk at this time. In the first issue, Hernández declares: "Punk: Not a fashion, more than just music; it's a lifestyle." Her unapologetic tone infuses the writings of a variety of contributors: from Erica Ortegón's account of a friend betraying her to Mikey Morales' column titled "Mikey says: You're Fucked (and tells you why, too)." Punk collage art infuses the issue, which even includes a cut out "Shimpies doll," a plug for Hernández's and Ortegón's band, the Shimpies.[48]

In her second issue, she calls for unity among Chuco punx, especially after the demise of the Rugburn. She intentionally released her second issue on March 17, 1997, to honor the National Day Against

Cover of Lindy Hernández's summer 1997 issue of her zine *Candy from Strangers*

Police Brutality. Her forcefulness about inequality and police brutality takes an even more passionate tone as she calls for Chuco punx to keep the spirit alive, even after the Rugburn came to an end. Hernández exclaims that whatever role a punk wants to take to keep the scene alive, it was worth it. She emphasized, "Let everyone out there know that El Paso DOES have a punk scene."[49]

Jenny Cisneros's *Pure Cheese* (or *Puro Queso*), by contrast, is a fusion of essays on animal rights and a celebration of punk fun and love. Cisneros inserts a picture of the first ear grown from a mouse's body with a screaming Snoopy yelling into a word bubble, "What the fuck?! Is this the value humans place on creatures of the Earth?" The serious condemnation is prefaced with a light review of young punk love, where Cisneros gushes in her zine about her boyfriend "babysitting [her] guinea pig while she leaves town," and "him being an anarchist, [her] being a cheesarchist."

On the back cover, Cisneros drew a crying cholo named "Tecato." Her illustration is indicative of the broader fluidity of Chuco punk, where cholas/cholos and metal heads were also intertwined in the culture.[50] Moreover, it points to the broader influence of cholo culture on Chuco punk, reaffirming the uniquely Mexican nature of this scene.

Feminism and gender studies scholar Alison Piepmeier asserts that grrrl zines of the 1990s reflect the experience of girlhood and also "offer idiosyncratic, surprising, yet savvy and complex responses to late-twentieth century incarnations of sexism, racism, and homophobia."[51] These Chuceñas' zines can be seen as part of a wider movement of women, especially women of color like Hernández, that used zines as a powerful tool to disseminate unique ideas of fun, politics, and identity to a broader audience. More importantly, Reiser and Beard's feminism, Hernandez's calls for punk participation, and Cisneros' condemnation of animal cruelty illustrate the ways in which Chuco punk culture was a space for a variety of perspectives and experiences among women.

The expectations of traditional masculinity in punk style proved equally problematic. Franko Tormenta says he "started looking crazy" in eighth grade, and his first stylistic transgression was the length of his hair. One day, Tormenta remembers his dad telling him, "Ya cabrón! Ya te toca el corte de pelo. I'm like, "Ya no me lo voy a cortar." What ensued was a fistfight between Tormenta and his father, the result of which led Tormenta to never cut his hair again. Moreover, as a young gay teen, like with the girls, acceptance among skaters, and later punx, was always dicey. Therefore, his close friends were always cholas or rocker girls who fully embraced him.

Navigating issues of masculinity was also a challenge for Tony Leal, especially after he put up a poster on his bedroom wall of Glenn Danzig posing without his shirt. Most of the time, his parents tolerated what they saw as the "gospel del Diablo," but a poster of Glenn Danzig in the buff on Tony's wall was a step too far. Tony recounts, "My dad wanted me to take all my Diablo Shit down that day" so Leal complied. The next day, when he came home after school, his dad had left a rolled-up poster on Tony's bed. What eventually unfurled before Tony was a large poster of "Budweiser Girls" in the back of a pickup truck. The bottom of the poster read, "Haulin' Ass." Leal explains that he put the Budweiser poster away in his closet "with the rest of the yunque and then, the Diablo Shit went [back] up on the walls a couple of weeks later." He reflects his father is not a homophobe, but the poster conflict "probably had to do with that traditional Mexican macho upbringing he grew up with out there."

While the shared sense of connection through music was tangible in Chuco, the scene did not go untouched by the broader inequities pervasive throughout society, creating limitations and exclusions. Nevertheless, punk rock provided an open sense of space and the tools to express a broad spectrum of frustrations and identities.

As Chuco punx were grappling with the limitations of the scene's inclusiveness, ATDI's indefatigable approach to touring and vitriolic live performances were catapulting them into the national consciousness.

ACROBATIC TENEMENT

By 1996, Chuco punk was teeming with bands that were eager to perform and tour. ATDI was able to harness this intensity and land themselves a major-label record deal. ATDI's 1994 release *Hell Paso* was in no way successful. Decades later, Jim Ward reflected on the popularity of the EP: "It was a three song seven inch. It came out that fall for $3. We literally couldn't give them away. Literally. At one point we just called them the $3 coasters."[52] The band's unrelenting commitment to touring and their ruthlessly energetic live shows eventually began to pay off, though. *Flipside* writer Blaze James attended a show ATDI played to a crowd of nine people at Bob's Frolic III in Los Angeles. Impressed with the band's vertiginous energy and sound, he helped them record their first LP on *Flipside*'s label with a $600 budget in Los Angeles.[53] Although this LP was recorded miles away in California, the essence of Chuco permeated its lyrics and music.

Geographic markers emerge in songs like "Porfirio Díaz," which is an homage to Porfirio Díaz street in central El Paso. The song starts with a shout of "Kiss and Kill Your Boyfriends," which was also a departing tag Bixler-Závala left in the zine *Femme Fatale*. Bixler-Závala left the line after a page and a half diatribe against sexism and a call for women, his spelling was "womyn," to play in punk bands. He urged women in the scene to move beyond "hanging from their boyfriend's shoulders, or gaucking [*sic*] at the cute guys in the band."

Instead, he calls for girls to make themselves visible. In essence, he was calling for them to take to the stage and play in their own bands. In his signature style, Bixler-Závala left his concise, pithy, and cutting ending.

> Don't let the cool kids intimidate you. Womyn have the power. . . .
> Kiss and Kill Your Boyfriends![54]

More somber in tone was the song "Embroglio," which mourns the February 1996 suicide of a friend and bandmate of Bixler-Závala's in the band Phantasmagoria. The twenty-three-year-old Julio Venegas committed suicide by jumping off an Interstate 10 overpass. While not struck by any cars, he was pronounced dead on arrival at Thomason Hospital.[55] In the song "Embroglio," ATDI pays homage to Venegas:

> I had a friend who died
> For something he really loved
> I had a friend who stood
> For none of the above . . .
> I had a friend, but now
> He's stranded on the Mesa Street Exit.
> I had a friend whose heart was too heavy to hold
> Yes there is blood on the median
> Like a boat without oars.[56]

The snapshots of this album placed side-by-side create a panorama of the Chuco punk experience and, for the first time, a broader audience was paying attention. While *Acrobatic Tenement* was a milestone for the band, it was also indicative of the entire scene's tireless work setting up their own labels, shows, and venues to create such a hot synergy that it was inevitable people outside of El Paso would eventually notice.

> **We're the Ones Having Fun Dancing for the Weather**
> You can tell us we're so primitive
> Why don't we get it together

But we're the ones having fun
Dancing for the weather
Sbitch, "Satisfy the Instinct," Satisfy the Instinct *(Self-released, 2001)*[57]

Second generation punx brought a particular energy, tenacity, and commitment to fun and community to the city. While there were certainly hierarchies, animosities, *chisme*, and *mamadas*, the guiding focus was not money or prestige, but a desire to create and connect. Their refusal inspired not only raw and invigorating music, but a creative drive to reconfigure their city and their relationships to serve music, and this second generation did just that. Punx upended municipal, state, and international borders. They reconfigured tame backyards and car repair shops throughout the city, in Juárez and Las Cruces, into dynamic sites of sound, creativity, and belonging. The cartography they practiced embedded geographic markers like that in ATDI's first full-length album, *Acrobatic Tenement.*

They did this all with a rascuache ethos that was also a form of innovation rooted in Mexican culture. Chicana novelist and poet Sandra Cisneros defines rascuache as "the term for making something from readily available materials. An old tire transformed into a planter. A shed patched with hubcaps. A toy airplane made from a beer can. Poverty is the mother of invention."[58] Chuco punx harnessed this ingenuity that was rooted in their own traditions as they cobbled together shows out of the desert and zines out of pilfered Kinko's copies.

Chuco punx' geographic wanderings and rascuache creativity also fueled their part in sparking the Latinx Hardcore Revolution of the '90s. Bands Revolución X, Sbitch, and Second Hand Human gave voice to anger on a spectrum of issues in the '90s: environmental devastation, economic upheaval, and racism. Chuco punk became just as important to Latinx Hardcore punk as bands in Chicago or New York City. Collectively, their sound and message underlined that punx of color, like those in Chuco, are integral to punk rock's heritage.

Jenny Cisneros's extraterrestrial howling as the frontwoman for Sbitch illustrates the role women played in Latinx Hardcore and the more visible and pervasive roles they played in the second generation of Chuco punk. On stage you had Laura Beard, Sara Reiser, Lindy Hernández and others simultaneously throwing shows and furiously creating their own zines. Second generation punkeras were definitely chingonas, and while some expressed frustration with the limitations they saw in the scene and in society broadly, they used punk rock as a tool of resistance to push back against those gendered limitations.

This was a pivotal time, and as Chuco punk started to come to national attention toward the end of the '90s, there was still surprise that this seemingly city of the "Wild West" could even produce such creativity. Sbitch's "Satisfy the Need" provides a clear retort. Despite being seen as primitive, Jenny Cisneros sings, "But we're the ones having fun/Dancing for the weather." Their commitment to punk and unfettered fun and passion reconfigured the city and left a lasting mark of punk for generations to come.

As the calendar turned to January 1, 1997, Chuco punx began to realign their trajectories away from home. In the next five years, the twists and turns of this journey forever transformed the city, and these punx were never the same afterwards.

4

"THIS IS FOREVER"

Indelible Chuco

Our bodies are not our voices
Or our outlets to the world.
Our minds are what matter.
Our minds are what you hear

Sarah Reiser, 1996, Femme Fatale zine

Strum this Broken Harp
We were struck by the chords sent from their hearts
Yes, this is forever.
March 23rd
This is forever.

At the Drive-In, "Napoleon Solo," In/Casino/Out *(Fearless Records, 1998)*

THE DRIVE FROM AUSTIN TO El Paso is an arduous one. Although tied like an umbilical cord musically, the 575 miles of geographic distance makes this a long, exhausting trek.

For Sara Reiser and Laura Beard, this route was a familiar one.

By 1997, El Paso could no longer contain Chuco punx' energy, as bands intensified their touring throughout the US. Many were also uprooting and moving to cities like Albuquerque, Oakland, and Austin, where Reiser and Beard were visiting friends in late March.

By the 23rd, it was then time for the seventeen-year-old punx to head back home with another one of their friends. They jumped into their Nissan pickup and merged onto I-10, heading west for home.

At approximately 7:09 a.m., the driver fell asleep at the wheel, drifting into the left lane of the freeway, a little more than thirty miles east from El Paso. The driver overcorrected, the pickup rolled over, and Reiser and Beard were thrown from the vehicle and killed instantly.

ATDI's song "Napoleon Solo" was a searing tribute in the aftermath of this tragedy, mourning loss, and its finality, with journalists and punk historians inadvertently turning it into lyrical synecdoche for the vitality and dynamism of the girls' lives that the song intends to honor.

Reiser's and Beard's vigorous participation in Chuco punk was indicative of the transition the entire scene was undergoing in 1997.

Lower Valley punk Jason Cagann, who had been on the same road just a few hours ahead of Reiser and Beard on March 23, explains that while the pain of this loss was profound, it was also a unifying moment for a scene that had, until recently, been grappling with regional rivalries. "The Westside and the Lower Valley were united, so we kind of experienced [Reiser's and Beard's deaths] as a group.[1]

This move towards unity occurred simultaneously with the second generation of punx electrifying their sound and bringing it to a wider audience outside the confines of backyards in Chuco. The most vivid version of this sonic outreach was ATDI's 2000 release of *Relationship of Command*, which shook the complacent punk sensibilities of national audiences. Embedded in those complacent sensibilities were preconceptions of punk as white. ATDI's mere existence, and the predominantly brown Chuco punk scene that birthed it, shattered those facile preconceptions with a type of innovative sound that advanced punk rock light years away from stale Blink-182 and the Offspring strain of pop-punk that was choking radio stations at the time.

Relationship of Command was not an isolated outburst of creativity. Chuco punk sound and ingenuity were everywhere. By the beginning of the twenty-first century, Chuco punx were taking to the airwaves, MTV, bars, and even the cover of their beloved *Maximum*

Rocknroll. Chuco punx assumed the means of communication and sound and were reworking it in their own image, not only musically, but also politically, as they worked to address the mass murder of women and girls along the border. Although radiating in so many different directions, punx' connection to their hometown did not dissipate, but evolved and became more pronounced. All the while, the core was an effort for music and words to transcend the present and forge an ever-enduring connection and community, despite borders and boundaries.

As the third generation of Chuco punx were springing up, the second generation, especially Chicanas, were growing bolder and more poised in their exploits. Some were heading off to Austin or Denver, but many like Marina Monsisvais and Marissa Chávez had their hometown in their sights. Along with first generation punk Bobbie Welch, they came together to organize the Mujer Festival to shed light on the femicides occurring along the border and to raise funds for Juárez's only domestic violence shelter, Casa Amiga. This festival harnessed the rascuache ethos of Chuco punx from a variety of generations with all their energy and focus on social justice. The sound and passion of the time didn't signal an endpoint, but rather a time when Chuco punk was evolving into something different and more powerful.

Sarah Reiser understood Chuco punk's expansive potential years earlier, in 1996. In her zine *Femme Fatale* that she created along with Laura Beard and Leah Lloyd, Reiser wrote a column about the pernicious nature of sexism in society. Her words can also be seen as an insight into the perennial nature of creativity from this punk scene.

Our bodies are not our voices, or our outlets to the world.
Our minds are what matter.
Our minds are what you hear[2]

Reiser and Beard were part of a Chuco punk scene that knew that sound and words did matter, and Reiser's and Beard's music and zines are like a topographical map that provides texture to the vital trajectory of their lives and their punk community.

Reiser had the foresight to acknowledge how Beard's and her enduring energy fed into Chuco punk right at the precipice of its explosion.

CIRCUIT OF MUSIC

That same year, Chuco punk Marina Monsisvais started attending college at New Mexico State University (NMSU), and she was hungry to bring punk to Las Cruces. Indeed, radiating this sonic frequency was integral to her mass communications major. NMSU had a college radio station, KRUX, and she wanted access to the station. Once she met fellow music lover Gustav "Guster" Verhulsdonck in class, all that was needed was the time slot. But they would have to pay their dues first.

The station manager told Monsisvais if she agreed to play country music once a week from 6 to 7 a.m. for one semester, a punk show was hers. After groggy mornings of Shania Twain and Clint Black, she and Guster seized the ideal Friday 8 p.m. to 10 p.m. slot for their *Underground Punk* show. They immediately transformed it into a forum for classic punk, pop punk, emo, and indie music, featuring the likes of more local New Mexican punk bands like the Eyeliners and nationally known bands like Jawbreaker, Face to Face, and the Get Up Kids. It also became a crucial way to connect punx in town to the live music culture in El Paso. On their way south to play in El Paso, bands stopped in Cruces for Monsisvais and Guster to interview on air. They also announced the El Paso shows, so the NMSU students could shoot down I-25 for live music. Even when Chuco punx left town, their commitment to disseminating sound, connection, and passion was firm.

It was clear to Monsisvais at that point: "We became part of a circuit of music."

Another long-standing part of this circuit of music was the Headstand, Chuco's foundational music store, but it was much more than that. It was a focal point of musical knowledge, inspiration, and congregation that fueled a variety of sonic revolutions, including Chuco punk. Founder and owner of the Headstand Stan Stack sold local punk music to young punx and hired generations of punx, including

Marina Monsisvais and Ted Telles, hosts of *Stepping Out* radio show

Chicanas like Monsisvais, who had a side gig there while attending NMSU.[3]

From the late '90s to the early 2000s, going to the Headstand continued to be a musical pilgrimage for second generation punx and the up-and-coming third generation. Franko Tormenta, for instance, lived almost twenty miles away, but he was determined to find Patti Smith tapes and other music. He was a devotee, so he skipped school, made the long walk to the closest bus stop, and then took the long ride to Northeast El Paso. The journey was worth it for Tormenta because it was the only place he could find the music he loved and discover new sounds.

It also became a hub of live music networking since Stack let punx leave flyers for shows at the shop. Lindy Hernández consistently left flyers when she was working for Fill Heimer's local label OOFAS! Records, flyers that ten-year-old punk Mike Hernández (no relation) was picking up because the Headstand "was the only place to go for information about shows."

Although the Headstand continued to be an enduring touchstone of music in the late '90s and early 2000s, live music venues were undergoing a sea change. In Juárez, for instance, the relationship between El Paso and Lencho's Place began to fizzle out around 1999 and 2000. A concomitant shift in El Paso was also occurring away from backyards to clubs and bars. Part of it was that the second generation was aging out of backyard shows. As Lower Valley punk Angel Iturbe puts it, "If you're twenty-eight years old hanging with kids at a backyard party, it's not a cool look." This overall feeling can be seen in the decline of Chuco bands appearing in *Book Your Own Fuckin' Life*. In 1997, for instance, nine out of forty-seven Texas bands were from Chuco,[4] but in 2001, only five were from Chuco, largely because they had moved to formal venues where booking bands was not in the hands of the punx themselves.[5]

This second generation then started playing in and going to shows at established venues like Club 101, Peanut Gallery, Moontime Pizza, and the Attic. But it would be a group of second generation punx that helped to establish Cantina La Tuya, one of the most important live music venues at this time.

Lower Valley punk Davey Lucey was one of the younger punx from the second generation who saw key show organizers like Ernesto Ybarra and Fill Heimer leave for Albuquerque and Salt Lake City. Before Ybarra and Heimer left town, they shared their knowledge of how to book shows, and Lucey was ready to set off on his own. In particular, he knew that the constant problem of cops busting backyard shows needed to be solved, so Lucey started looking for an alternative, which he found with local bar owner Rich Wright.

Wright owned Wildhare's, a local bar which put on primarily rockabilly and blues shows, and Lucey asked him to book other shows at Wildhare's. The timing was ideal because Wright had just started a foray with a sports bar called Cantina La Tuya. Lucey started bartending at Wildhare's, and eventually brought his friends Jessica Flores, Luis Mota, and Barry Peterson to book punk shows at La Tuya. During this era, Lucey continued helping Wright bring acts like Long John Hunter and John Lee Hooker to Wildhare's. Promoters at La Tuya brought music to El Paso and ensured that local punx could have a safe and undisturbed place to rock out. Lucey, Flores, Mota, and Peterson brought bands like the Eyeliners, the Ataris, UK Subs, T.S.O.L, and Cursive to town. Mota and Peterson also joined forces to book throughout the city with their new booking agency called Full Flavor

More than a special place to see shows, La Tuya changed the face of booking in Chuco. During the first wave of punk, major promoters of bars, clubs, and arenas, like Bobbie Welch, Mike Jennings, and Joe Dorgan, were all white. Welch and Jennings had college degrees, and Dorgan had attended UTEP for a time. During the second wave, on the other hand, you have primarily Chicanx kidz like Flores. Musicologist

David Pearson observes that throughout the country in the '90s, "the punk scene provided training in collective action [and] DIY activity."[6] Such Chuco punk training involved watching older friends throw shows, which sharpened their skills to start booking shows at clubs and bars later in their lives.

The transformation of venues and promoters also nourished a new sound in Chuco by the late 1990s. Angel Iturbe, a second-generation punk who bridged the backyard to club/venue era, puts his finger on this phenomenon. The new garage punk band Electric Funeral he started in 2000 had access to an entirely different range of equipment and feeling than when he played backyards with the Belvederes. Having access to a proper stage and equipment was transformative. "There you are, living out your Motley Crüe dream. You put your boot on the PA, and [now] you're playing all *mamón*."

Iturbe's evolving sound and performances in his two bands were indicative of larger tectonic movements of sound occurring throughout Chuco by the late '90s and early 2000s. Edmundo Valencia observed that in Juárez, the younger kids were more enamored with electronic music than with punk, and in El Paso, hardcore made way for more pop-punk, garage, and post-rock sounds. In the 1997 issue of *Book Your Own Fuckin' Life*, only one band, Second Hand Human, specifically described themselves as hardcore.[7] The few other Chuco bands described themselves as "pop-punk," "rock n' roll and very emotional," or "punk band with emo influence." This was absolutely a shift from the short, fast, and politically charged hardcore punk rock that had previously dominated the scene. For musicologist David Pearson, pop-punk is a "more palatable and melodic style of punk," epitomized by bands like Green Day.[8] Music critic and author Jessica Hopper pins down the sometimes elusive definition of emo-punk, a subgenre made popular by bands like Dashboard Confessional, as "the genre/plague" comprising songs "laden with the relational eulogies-hopeful boys with their hearts masted to sleeves, their pillows soaked in tears."[9] Bands such as Pragmatic, who described themselves as a "fast and melodic power pop band out of the land of salsa," and Wednesday, who wrote that they play "Jawbreaker style music, hits you where your lover doesn't," were the harbingers of this new wave of sound to emerge from Chuco.[10]

Another such band was Mikey Morales' Siva. No longer playing the hardcore of Lower Valley's VBF, Morales and company defined themselves as radically different, even from their pop-punk peers. On their website, their description was poetic and verbose. With a hint of punk rock snark, they described their sound as "a conscious deviation from the resurgence of nut-tugging garage bands and flaccid, radio-friendly pop punk. Classifying Siva as a post-rock five-piece would be like understanding magma as 'pretty.'" The nod to Chuco roots is explicit, even if their lovelorn focus is a facsimile of their *carnalas* and *carnales* in pop punk bands like Pragmatic and Wednesday: "[SIVA] is the chaos and confusion brought on by a border economy hanging on the edge of the Asarco smokestack. It's the sting of a lover's name that you can't get off your mind at 3 a.m."[11] Indeed, the ever-present Chuco permeates SIVA's identity.

Another band appearing in *Book Your Own Fuckin' Life* with the nondescript "Write us and we'll send you something back," was Egon.[12] Music critic Peter D'Angelo found that Egon's sound "defies simple categorization . . . from arty intros to punk rock crescendos."[13] In 1999, Lauren Cisneros started playing bass for the band. Unlike many other punx, she became part of the punk community later on when she was in college at UTEP. Once Lauren started going to shows, she was encouraged by the presence of other girls in the scene, the majority of whom were supportive of her. She was similarly inspired when she played her first show in Las Vegas, Nevada. Even though Lauren knew only a few songs, she went out and played. "There were a bunch of kids out there, like teens. They were cheering me on! Even though it was not ideal, everyone was like, 'Hey! You did it!'" Fellow musicians, however, were not always as supportive. Some male musicians saw it as their duty to quiz her on music knowledge. From her perspective, they were trying to gauge whether or not she was "punk enough."

Despite the cynical evaluation of Lauren's punk rock points, her fellow female Chuco punk, Jenny Cisneros (no relation to Lauren),

Jenny Cisneros, lead singer of Sbitch, blazes *MMR*'s August 2001 cover

reached the apogee of underground punk rock status. In 1995, Sbitch appeared among over forty other Texas bands with half-inch ads, describing themselves merely as "Pissed off brutal male/female vocals with a lot of attitude. SPIT."[14]

A mere six years later, a full-page photo of Jenny Cisneros howling into the microphone blazed the cover of *MMR*'s 2001 issue, bringing all the spunky and snarky ads for local labels and bands like Sbitch full circle. Sbitch had already relocated to Austin by this time, no longer with Alex Martínez, but still fronted by Jenny, with Jason Cagann on drums. Although deeply immersed in the music scene in Austin, Chuco is like a specter in the interview. When asked about the music scene in Austin, one band member declares how Austin is so much better than El Paso. However, Jenny interjects to give a shout out to Chuco afterwards: "There's actually quite a cool little scene in El Paso, and since I'm from there, I've got to give props to my homies."[15]

As the twentieth century came to an end, the Chuco circuit of music moved beyond the confines of the city and defied the limits of musical creativity. Their sound evolved into various directions, and at the helm were more Chicanas and Chicanos who were using their training throwing shows at the Rugburn or in backyards to host this new punk sound in bars like Cantina La Tuya. Chicanas like Marina Monsisvais, who hosted punk radio shows, and Jessica Flores, a key promoter at Cantina La Tuya, were essential architects of this scene as they ensured that nobody could escape the Chucotown sound.

This tumultuously creative milieu of sound could no longer go unnoticed outside of Chuco. Almost a year earlier, Sbitch's friends in ATDI had released their punk-shattering *Relationship of Command* on a major label, garnering a notoriety that contrasted with Sbitch's underground *MMR* acclaim. The band, however, developed a conflicted relationship with this unprecedented wave of attention. While the band's sound was embraced, its values were not, transforming their meteoric success into a grinding, and eventually destructive, experience.

"YOU'RE NOT PUNK, AND I'M TELLING EVERYONE!"

With a burgeoning new generation chomping at the bit, ATDI continued to charge through with more LPs as they honed their skills and sound but struggled to find a label to sign them. With Blaze James as their new manager, his efforts to get Fat, Epitaph, or Sub Pop to pick up ATDI fell flat. Ward's desire for Jade Tree, and Bixler-Závala's longing for Kill Rock Stars, were also just that: dreams. Fearless Records did eventually take a chance on the Chueños, and after *Acrobatic Tenement*, they released *In/Casino/Out* and *Vaya* on the label, which sold 10,000 records, and ATDI became Fearless's most popular band. Their underground success soon caught the attention of major labels.[16]

ATDI had finally reached the big time, and while they were not opposed to signing to a major label, the ancillary trappings of this "success" were going to become more and more unpalatable for many in the band.

In 1999 the major label deal was finally realized as ATDI signed a deal with Digital Entertainment Network Music Group. Immediately, the deal went up in smoke when Marc Collins-Rector, the chairman and founder, resigned after being sued for sexually assaulting a thirteen-year-old, which resulted in a large-scale investigation that revealed a history of abuse. The Beastie Boys' Mike Diamond saved the day and picked up the band for their Grand Royal record label, and the epic *Relationship of Command* was released on September 12, 2000.[17]

And nothing would be the same.

Critical acclaim for *Relationship of Command* was swift. Just five years earlier, they were promoting themselves like this:

"Happiness is a by-product of function." Got the patience? Watch us tick, a prescription of suggestion as the fuse grows shorter; !Bombard! We come to dance on the boredom of your unimpressed friends. Swim, sink or learn![18]

Six years later, *Relationship of Command* came in #5 in *Spin*'s "Top 20 Albums of 2000," outpacing PJ Harvey, Le Tigre, and U2. Reviewer Mike Rubin did not hold back, declaring:

Down in the West Texas town of El Paso, five guys discover the secret formula for breathing life back into rock's rotting corpse is E(mo)= MC5 . . . capable of evoking the ferocious power of a mushroom cloud.[19]

Indeed, the album's insatiable appetite for mercurial sound and energy are unprecedented, but the overall arrangement and momentum create a singular experience with the album. The first track, "Arcarsenal," lures the listener into an impending confrontation with sinister drumming and guitars. Subsequent tracks like "One Armed Scissor" absolutely erupt with ATDI's signature power, but the almost stalking approach that accompanies such shattering explosions makes the album a masterpiece. The third track from the end, "Cosmonaut," grabs you viscerally at 2:25 as it hypnotically repeats, "Is it heavier than air? / Am I supposed to die alone?" At 2:45 you are hurled off a sonic cliff into Cedric's deliciously frantic and cathartic screech as the drums, bass, and guitar bring this emotional flight to a halt like a gravitational pull.

ATDI had produced a classic, and their *carnales* back home knew it.

Chuco promoter Pantaleón Mena remembers that one moment ATDI was one of his favorite local bands, and all of a sudden, "One Armed Scissor" was being played on the same radio stations as Led Zeppelin and Nickelback. For him and others, the response was a clear: "No Fucking Way!"

Not all Chuco punx were so giddy about ATDI's good fortune, though. ATDI emerged from a punk scene, with anti-corporate/anti-major label stances as part and parcel of the culture. Therefore, it is not surprising that the band was immediately subject to what Green Day endured when *Dookie* was released in 1994. In 1998, *Profane Existence* writer joel wrote, "When punks get big, of course, the scene pretty much loses respect for them. (It was punks, after all, who painted "FUCK GREEN DAY" in huge letters on Gilman Street's walls after they released "Dookie." Not that I blame them.)"[20] Lower Valley punk Tony Leal observed the same level of "Hatorade getting served around" back home in Chuco for ATDI for precisely the same reasons

Green Day and Jawbreaker faced backlash: ATDI were signed to a major label.

As discouraging as this "Hatorade" was from the punk scene, the unwelcome element in the growing crowds, security, and professional stage crews at their new concerts was much more grueling. For Bixler-Závala and Ward, who were used to the "nerdy riot grrrls and the meek" in their audiences, they were soon overwhelmed by the "infestation of bros"[21] there to make ATDI sets a focal point of senseless, posturing, gendered violence. A harbinger of this juncture occurred when Zach de la Rocha and Tom Morello from Rage Against the Machine asked ATDI to join them for an arena tour. This opportunity immediately became a curse as Rage fans hurled pennies, nickels, copies of ATDI CDs, and homophobic epithets at ATDI as they attempted to play their sets.[22] Crew and stage managers matched this level of brutality. On a different tour, a security guard punched Rodríguez-López in the face before a show and dragged him out of the venue by his hair. At a KROK Los Angeles show with the likes of No Doubt and Moby playing, Papa Roach's security team mistakenly assaulted Jim Ward, and a woman continued to pull at Bixler-Závala's hair, accusing him of wearing a wig.[23]

Straining under all of this weight, the January 26, 2001, Big Day Out debacle appears inevitable for a band rooted in authenticity and talent, but scoured by the confluence of these forces. Three songs into the set, a flashpoint occurred when the band members started witnessing men in the audience punching women. Decades later, Rodríguez-López touches on the tenor of the times: "It was cool to be stupid and misogynist. That was the trend."[24]

This wasn't the "trend" for ATDI. They walked off stage and eventually broke up the band.

The drama in Australia had a delayed playback three months later back in Chuco, where the band's internal fissures were still raw and becoming increasingly apparent. Pantaleón Mena was working with Bobbie Welch and Joe Dorgan booking shows at Club 101 at the time, and he became the point man to bring Fugazi to Chuco. This was an iconic show at a pivotal time in the club's history. Even though Mena was usually in charge of booking industrial and metal bands at the club, Fugazi was his charge this time. In true DIY form, Ian MacKaye worked directly with Mena to set up the show, which meant that the club could only charge $6 a pop, and the opening band would have to share their equipment with Fugazi because they would not be traveling with their own gear.

Another key stipulation of MacKaye's was that the opening band had to be a good one that was *not* on a major label. Bixler-Závala and Rodríguez-López's jazz/salsa/rock sideband De Facto were booked to open. Once Fugazi came to the stage, the interpersonal rupture within ATDI was apparent. Bixler-Závala and Rodríguez-López watched from one side of the stage, and Ward, Hinojos, and Hajjar watched from the other. For Mena, it was a weird sight that was symbolic of the fissure that had developed.

The consensus among music critics frames the breakup as a shocking and squandered opportunity, but it was neither. The band could never have reconciled their firmly rooted ethos of feminism, ethnic pride, and non-violence with the vicious and predatory nature of the mainstream music business, a dilemma which further frayed interpersonal tensions within the band. Furthermore, the end of ATDI did not stifle the raging creativity that was the allure of their music in the first place. Rodríguez-López and Bixler-Závala were already active in De Facto by early 2001, and The Mars Volta's first EP *Tremulant* was released in April of 2002, just a year after ATDI's dissolution. Meanwhile, Hinojos, Hajjar, and Ward started the band Sparta and released their ferocious album *Wiretap Scars* in August of 2002. As poet and music critic Hanif Abdurraqib has observed, listeners are able to hear and feel in *Relationship of Command* all of the powerful countervailing sonic forces in ATDI, without muting "Bixler-Zavala's lyrics, nor Rodríguez-López's soaring guitar visions, nor Ward's insistence on volume."[25] Indeed, the 2001 breakup simply opened the floodgates for these volatile and resplendent progressions to immediately take their natural sonic courses.

As jarring as the fragmentation of ATDI was, it paled in comparison to the militarization and violence engulfing the border at the time. All the changes, inequities, and contradictions that had evolved in the 1990s had turned especially poisonous by 2000, threatening the long-standing connection between Juárez and El Paso.

"AND A SILENCING THAT STILL WALKS THE STREETS . . ."

Political scientist Peter Andreas describes photos of the Tijuana/ San Diego border in 1991. For him, distinguishing features included crowds of people milling in front of an unguarded chain link fence, "seemingly oblivious that the border even exists." Almost a decade later, a ten-foot-high metal fence, Border Patrol officers, and an absence of the milling crowds had eclipsed the supposedly "defied, defeated, and underfunded" border of the early 1990s.[26] A turning point had occurred not only in Tijuana/San Diego, but all along the border, threatening to sever tight connection between *las ciudades gemelas*: Juárez and El Paso.

Silvestre Reyes's Operation Blockade started in 1993. This over-haul was just the first step in a radical transformation to border enforcement, reverberating both nationally and internationally. Reyes's strategy was further bolstered by the end of the Cold War in 1989 as national security priorities shifted away from anticommunism to stemming the tide of narcotics into the United States, especially along the Mexican/US border. Therefore, increased investment in border enforcement was soon visible everywhere along the border. Between 1995 and 2001, the federal budget for the Immigration and Naturalization Services (INS) tripled, and by 2002, it had reached a staggering $2.5 billion. A clear indicator of this change was that by 2000, the INS had more employees authorized to carry guns than any other federal law enforcement agency.

Reyes developed the strategy known as "Operation Blockade" with help from the Pentagon's Center for Low Intensity Conflict, so it was no surprise that military forces were soon a conspicuous force with the INS along the international border. In the 1990s, the US Army,

National Guard, and Marine Corps participated in 3,000 drug and immigration-related missions along the border,[27] their headquarters located at El Paso's Fort Bliss.[28]

US citizens were immediately caught in the literal crossfire of border militarization, most visibly in 1997. Aiding the Border Patrol was a Marine unit that was on a covert drug-patrol mission near Redford, Texas. On May 20, 1997, US citizen and high school sophomore Esequiel Hernández was herding goats near Redford. Marine Clemente Bañuelos mistook Esequiel for a threat because the eighteen-year-old was supposedly brandishing a rifle to protect his goats. With one shot, Bañuelos killed Esequiel, a murder that did not go unnoticed by Chuco punk Lindy Hernández (no relation to the victim).[29] In her zine *Candy From Strangers*, she is scathing in her column, "The Killers of Esequiel Hernandez Went Free & No One Cares!!!" Esequiel's murder exemplifies what she sees as the US government's empty gestures to "solve" the problem of undocumented immigration. She decried this senseless killing of a Mexican American teenager and was appalled that in the predominantly Mexican El Paso, nobody seemed to care about the murder. She ends with chilling questions, "So do I have a reason for getting worked up about this? OR should I assimilate to the rest of society and turn my cheek?"[30]

The urgency of Lindy's outrage was timely as such violence was not only occurring on the US side of the border but was also consuming Mexican border communities in the late '90s and early 2000s. The causes of such violence were multiple, complex, and vicious.

The passage of the North American Free Trade Agreement (NAFTA) in 1994, first of all, opened up trade throughout North America, unintentionally clearing the way to expanded drug trafficking, too. In 1993, Amado Carrillo Fuentes assumed control of the market in Juárez, making the city home to the largest drug cartel in Mexico. The cartel was so powerful that Carillo was instrumental in importing 70 percent of all cocaine that entered the US in the '90s. Carrillo died in 1997 while undergoing cosmetic surgery in Mexico City, and a vicious turf war exploded among 450 rival gangs in Juárez vying for control of the drug trade. In her book *The Daughters of Juárez: The True Story of*

Serial Murder South of the Border, journalist Teresa Rodríguez writes of the devastating consequences: "With Carrillo's passing, the drug war had escalated to a level not seen before. In the past, the killings had been confined to individuals in the trade. Now innocent bystanders were being picked off if they got in the way."[31]

Many such innocent bystanders were found in the burgeoning workforce that NAFTA spurred. Border factories, or maquiladoras, grew in number, and women made up about half of the 250,000 strong workforce at the peak of maquila growth.[32] Many of these women were recruited from areas in Southern Mexico and Central America with the promise that they would be paid $1,000 every two weeks. Eventually, the companies brought buses of these young women to work in Juárez. Sometimes, these women were as young as fifteen years old and were often dumped in Juárez with nowhere to live.[33] These women and girls were immediately caught up in pervasive gang violence and economic precarity, two of the forces which led to an explosion of femicides along the border.

While pioneering *El Paso Times* journalist Diana Washington Valdez defined femicides as "gender murders,"[34] the head of the National Citizen Femicide Observatory, Maria de la Luz Estrada, explains, "Hate is what marks these crimes. The bodies show twenty or thirty blows."[35] Indeed, from 1993 to 2003, Amnesty International estimated that 370 such femicides took place in Juárez.[36] Seventy-five of the victims were never identified, and that does not touch upon the six hundred women that had simply disappeared from Juárez and Cd. Chihuahua in this era.[37]

Despite the severity and explosion in the number of femicides, police authorities systematically downplayed the murders, ignored the pleas of desperate families, or impugned the reputation of the victims, asserting that they were promiscuous women that invited their own demise. Moreover, when the governor of the state of Chihuahua created a Special Task Force for the Investigation of Crimes Against Women in 1998, the director, Suly Ponce Prieto, came to realize that police had burned thousands of pounds of evidence. Her office had been cleared of files related to previous investigations, and bystanders and news reporters had been given unlimited access to crime scenes, making reliable evidence retrieval virtually impossible.[38]

Since officials refused to document the femicides, Juárez activist Esther Chávez Cano started recording the data on the murdered and missing women and girls in 1993 by collecting newspaper clippings. While the numbers were essential, the pressing gendered violence also needed to be addressed, so she joined a group of thirteen other feminist organizations in Coordinadora de Organismos No Gubernamentales en Pro de la Mujer. The group both advocated for the prosecution of the femicides and sought ways to prevent them. In 1999, Chávez Cano opened Casa Amiga, a nonprofit counseling center, Juárez's only sanctuary for those facing domestic and family violence.[39] Casa Amiga offered, and continues to offer, medical treatment, therapy, legal assistance, and safe houses to victims of such violence.[40]

Chávez Cano was not alone, as activists in both Juárez and El Paso began to engage in public demonstrations to honor the victims and bring the problem to the community's attention. The mothers of the slain women and girls set the tone. Victims were referred to as "daughters," and the rallying cry "Ni una más" was heard at protests on both sides of the border. Pink and black crucifixes and sometimes photos of the missing girls and women appeared on walls, telephone poles, and major streets, serving as potent reminders of the victims and also the impunity of the perpetrators.[41]

Chuco punx brought their distinctive ways to combat this injustice to the fore, too. Although they recorded the album in Malibu on a major label, ATDI's song "Invalid Litter Dept." and the accompanying video memorialize the victims in Juárez, shed light on the issue, and eviscerate Mexican and American unwillingness to hold anybody accountable.

In contrast to Bixler-Závala's usual kaleidoscopically opaque lyrics, "Invalid Litter Dept." delivers straightforward images of the slayings and the impunity of the murderers and complicit officials. When journalists first reported on the femicides, photos of the victims' shoes thrown in the desert symbolized the disposability presumed by the murderers of the victims. The song immediately evokes iconic images of the anonymity of these murders. For instance, the sudden introduction of "these shoes gripped on the ballroom floor/in the silhouette of dying," forces the listener's focus on these murders and does not allow it to stray with the repeated refrain of "dancing on the corpses ashes" throughout the song. It then moves to excoriate Mexican officials' perfunctory efforts, such as "cobblestone curfews" for young women in Juárez, to stem the tide of femicides, without legitimately addressing the perpetrators who were a "silencing that still walks the streets." The lyrical allusions to the murders eventually collide with the emotional pit these massacres leave, and the song lurches at 4:35 in repeated "dancing on the corpses ashes," unaccompanied by music. At 4:47 you are met with a sonic blast of Ward's and Rodríguez-López's guitars and Cedric's mournful, "callous heels/numbed in travel/endless maps made by their scalpel," only punctuated eventually with Cedric's extended and mournful howl.[42]

The music video was similarly intentional in its focus, evolving into more of a documentary than popular culture pabulum. Without question, the band took the preparation for this video seriously. Cedric first reached out to his father, Dr. Dennis Bixler-Márquez, Director of Chicano Studies at University of Texas at El Paso (UTEP), when planning the video. In an interview with the UTEP's newspaper *The Prospector*, Dr. Bixler-Márquez explains, "He [Cedric] called me when they decided to shoot the video. We talked about it. I told him it was a very delicate subject," Bixler-Márquez said. "They told me through their music they wanted to raise a consciousness of what's going on in Juárez."[43] The video did just that. The first image is of one of the commemorative crosses painted on a telephone pole and soon followed by a map of Juárez/El Paso with the first of many similarly informative subtitles declaring information like, "Since 1993, scores of women have been murdered in Juárez, Mexico." In the video the band is shown intermittently throughout Juárez and in El Paso, but the images of the maquilas, the border, photos of victims' shoes, and the crosses to commemorate the women and girls, not the band, are preeminent. Indeed, the band members only appear sporadically throughout the six-minute video for a total of fifty seconds, and when they do, they are either standing near open graves or near the crosses commemorating the women and girls' murders.[44] From the first scenes of road signs pointing to Juárez and El Paso, Texas, the undeniable presence not only of the Chuco sound, but of the horrors of femicide along the border were broadcast to a national audience.

The song and video were but two points in a broader and more powerful array of concerted and collective resistance to femicides. Lower Valley punk Marissa Chávez soon became an instrumental leader in this fight. After completing her BA in social work from University of Texas at Austin, Chávez became active on the UTEP campus in 2002. Her social justice activism at Lower Valley punk shows years before manifested into concerted social action over the femicides along the border. She met a few other students there who were also interested in feminist and gender politics and they created a chapter of the Feminist Majority Leadership Alliance on campus. Jessica Irimedi from Juárez was also involved in the chapter. She and Chávez began to organize several events around the femicides. She met other locals as well, such as Ruby Castro and Kiko Rodríguez, previously of Second Hand Human. At the time, Rodríguez was playing in the band FUGA!, who were also active politically. Chávez and others organized a variety of events to raise awareness and funds for Casa Amiga.

During one silent protest she organized on April 19, 2002, all the participants wore black and held up placards with pink and black crosses and signs to memorialize the murdered and missing women and girls. Attending the protest was fellow Chuco punk Jesus Portillo, whom Chávez had known from shows in the '90s. Portillo approached her and suggested that she have a concert to raise money for Casa Amiga. Chávez agreed, and the organizational wheels started spinning.

The nascent idea of a concert developed into plans for a full-on festival, and the three-month-long planning for the July 14 "Mujer Festival" was in the works.

The punk rock scene was the ideal machine to organize this festival, and Portillo seized all the levers at his disposal. He and his band the Fla Flas first created the organization M.U.J.E.R. (Musicians United for Justice, Equality, and Respect). This group was the central force of

Flyer for the 2002 Mujer Festival to raise funds for Casa Amiga in Juárez

organizing the event and became a Chuco punk brain trust with first and second generation punx all focused on promoting this cause.

Two of the most important people brought into M.U.J.E.R. were Bobbie Welch and Marina Monsisvais. When Welch joined, she asked Joe Dorgan to donate his space, and the "Club 101 Complex" became a site not only of sound, but also of education. Emerging from a social work background, education was to be central, and Chávez organized speakers from Juárez and the El Paso Center for Family Violence to take part in the event.

The educational component was not lost on first-generation punk and music promoter Bobbie Welch, either. The festival for her was about changing minds. Welch says, "Changing minds is such an important component of music, and you can do that somewhat from the stage, but a lot of times, people just nod along, and say, 'Fight the power!,' then go home, and then they discriminate, and they do stupid shit. . . . The educational component [of The Mujer Festival] was much more in your face."

Portillo was in charge of booking local bands like the Fla Flas, Siva, and Border Roots from El Paso, and also seeking bigger bands to headline. Two main bands proposed were Sparta and Ozomatli. Although Jim Ward's new band, Sparta, was on tour at the time, opening for Weezer, they agreed to make it back home in between the Detroit and Cleveland dates for the festival. With Sparta set, all that was left was Ozomatli. Kiko Rodríguez spoke with Raul Pacheco from the band and explained what was going on in Juárez and the plan to have the festival. Pacheco was convinced, but Kiko explained that the organizers could not afford to fly the entire band into El Paso. Ozomatli ended up playing for free and only requested that the organization cover the hotel costs and "a very basic per diem." For Welch, who was in charge of the finances, her experience with Ozomatli during The Mujer Festival was singular: it was the only time she had witnessed that level of generosity from a band in her decades of work in music.

Once the festival started on July 14, the energy and sense of purpose was everywhere. Welch and Monsisvais worked furiously, doing everything from setting out chairs to getting water for the bands. It was hard work, but as Welch notes: "We're women, and we're powerful. And we organized like hell!"

One of the first bands to play was Mikey Morales' band, Siva. Unfortunately, since he had just downed six cans of Red Bull, his memory of his own set is hazy, but not that of Ozomatli. Indeed, the show was transformative for the self-described "dumb garage rocker elitism" that made him disdainful of bands like Ozomatli. Once Ozomatli took the stage, he was a convert.

> Their set was interactive. The groove was HEAVY and thick on every song. At one point they got off the stage, leaving only the bass and drums to carry the feel, and the rest of them grabbed percussion instruments and went into the crowd. They formed an impromptu conga line and then brought everyone on stage for a free for all dance. It was beautiful.

As fun as the music was, the event was also deeply meaningful. As Morales explains, "The feeling of community and optimism [at The

Mujer Festival] was palpable." This feeling" had very tangible effects, too. Overall, the event raised $20,000 for Casa Amiga.[45]

What was also tangible at that moment was the power of punk rock.

When the *El Paso Times* interviewed Monsisvais about The Mujer Festival, she explained:

> We've really put our punk rock ethic to work with this cause. It was put together by young people for young people to tell everyone they can do something about what is happening in their backyard.[46]

It was clear that their rascuache punk rock ethic was still fully operational and was in fine form by the end of the twentieth century. Although the tragedy of femicide transcended international borders, so too did activism to stop it. Punk music and collaboration reached beyond international boundaries in the pursuit of the more just landscape of Chuco. Moreover, the punk community of the late '70s, '80s, and '90s proved a durable resource to dexterously maneuver the complex planning required of Mujer Fest, attesting to the lasting mark punk rock would make in this region.

CHUCO PUNK VS. OBLIVION

In 1998, Bixler-Závala and Rodríguez-Lopez refused to slick down their hair in pomade any longer. When it started to grow out, journalists were obsessed with it, and in 2000, Greg Kot at the *Chicago Tribune* even wrote that they "looked like human Q-Tips," but just like with the pachucos of the early twentieth century, style had a much deeper meaning. Bixler-Závala explained, "You know this if you're Puerto Rican, if you're Mexican, if you're Black. That's just you going, 'You know what? I'm tired of putting this shit in my hair. . . . For me, my homie's out here going natural. Why don't I just go natural?'"[47]

Right at this crucial cusp in Chuco punk's history, the most visible and iconic images of Chuco punk were of these two guys proudly brandishing their hair and ethnic pride to an increasingly national audience, a gesture that was not solitary, but resounding as Chuco punk took it to the next level. From Jenny Cisneros doing a shout-out to El Paso after making the cover of *MMR* to Lindy Hernández calling out the injustice of Esquiel Hernandez's murder, Chuco punk was louder and Browner than ever, illustrating that punk was never exclusively white, that it had always been Brown and down. And by the turn of the century, they were not toning this down, but rather amping it up.

Chicanas like Jessica Flores and Marina Monsisvais were especially eager to turn up the volume since their training in punk rock trenches in the nineties informed their poised operation of punk venues, radio stations, and music festivals in the early 2000s. They were at a powerful turning point where punx were bringing Chuco to the national level. Their sound and creativity was permeated with a more visible ethnic pride as well as a continual sense of devotion to their home.

There is no better example of that than the development of Mujer Fest. As a collaboration of different generations of punx, the focus on stemming injustice was key, and their rascuache ethos was an indispensable tools to make this event happen.

Mujer Fest was the apogee of Chuco punk collaboration and ingenuity and one of the many visible points from 1997 to 2002 in which these punx did not "just grow out of it" or grow silent after the end of relations and bands. Rather, they developed, matured, and used all the Chuco roots and knowledge to magnify all the creativity they had already cultivated and even more ferociously, more fervently, created new and innovative sounds, words, and connections.

It was an intoxicating time, but it was still rooted in home and community. With the backdrop of femicide in the late 1990s and early 2000s, remembering and documenting were the focal points of activism and creativity. Scholar Julia Monárrez Fragoso observes that since femicide becomes so prevalent, "the victims' names or where they were killed are forgotten from one day to the next. Forgetting is part of what those who remain observers or those agents who execute the aggression do. As opposed to the victim whose feelings and body are marked with everything she has to remember."[48]

Whether they were making sure Sara Reiser and Laura Beard were not forgotten or organizing The Mujer Festival, this generation of punx passionately struggled against such forgetting.

ATDI's most successful breakout tune, "One Armed Scissor," articulates the emotional undercurrent of this moment.

> Dissect a trillion sighs away
> Will you get this letter
> Jagged pulp sliced in my veins
> I write to remember[49]

While particular to one band and one song, this lyric is a powerful reflection of the passion, power, and sound of Chuco punx and their refusal to be erased. Moreover, it sheds light on how they used those talents for others without a voice because they were aware of the unique way music connects us beyond the present and does not allow us to forget.

CONCLUSION

"El Paso Is in Every One of Us!"

ON APRIL 25, 2022, CARLOS Palacios took the stage at El Paso's Lowbrow Palace, but not with the Sicteens.

The Sicteens have garnered an underground following internationally over the last twenty years. The Chuco punk band is especially popular in Australia, where the young "shred rock" band the Chats count themselves as some of the Sicteens' most devoted fans. They've even become close friends with Palacios over the years. On that warm Texas spring evening, Palacios was taking the stage with the Chats.

Palacios towered above the three Australians like a punk rock shaman, all in black with the Ramones-esque touches of sunglasses, a leather jacket, and a beer in hand.

The bassist, Eamon Sandwith, then introduced in his Aussie accent, "We're going to play a song from an old El Paso band called the Sicteens. They're from the early '90s."

The band then furiously launched into "A.P.B." with Palacios on lead vocals for the song he'd written decades before. When they arrived at the chorus, both the Chats and the frenetic Chuco audience were shouting "A.P.B!" "A.P.B!" "A.P.B!"[1]

The scope and depth of the connection between these two bands is profound, transcending geography and generations. The magnitude of it was not lost on Palacios at the time. He explains, "The fact that the Chats went out and found The Sicteens on their own, plus learned the tune while on tour at Coachella was mind blowing to me. Playing 'A.P.B' with [the Chats] felt like playing with the A-Team; it never sounded so good."

When The Sicteens were just starting twenty years earlier, Chuco punk's influence was simply a vision on the horizon for Alex Martínez writing in the *El Paso Punk Zine*. Martínez put out a call to arms and urged his fellow Chuco punx to stop fawning over the DC and San Francisco scenes. Instead, punx needed to readjust their focus back home and "start putting our ideas into action. . . . There's so much ground to be covered here! There are so many new things to be experimented with! Like my friend Nora put it, 'This is virgin territory for making a permanent dent for the punx!'"[2]

Martínez and others knew that Chuco was a special place for punk, and in the span of a few decades, punx cultivated this territory with music and community that shook the far reaches of the punk rock universe.

Its resonance and legacy are undeniable.

CHUCO PUNK IS PUNK AF

When you watch a 1973 recording of Tejano poet raúlsalinas reading his poem "Homenaje al Pachuco," you feel the rebellious and subversive beat of his epic poem. Donning a red bandana, sunglasses, and grey T-shirt, he almost dances as he gives homage to *pachuquismo* and where pachucos "sprang from EL CHUCO."[3]

Brown kids in early twentieth-century Juárez/El Paso cultivated the roots of *pachuquismo*, and Chuco punx were an extension of the region's legacy of cultural resistance, especially that of *pachuquismo*. And like with *pachuquismo*, Chuco punk's influence on sound and style is far-reaching, with ATDI being the most accessible illustration of Chuco punk's sway.

Poet and music critic Hanif Abdurraqib writes that ATDI are a rare breed in that they were "the architects of a sound that has evolved, without them. You can hear elements of ATDI in bands like Thursday and The Fall of Troy, or on the more emo side of things, influencing the music of bands like Pierce the Veil and Sleeping With Sirens." [4]

However, ATDI was but one chord in a broader composition that was interdependent, vibrant, and expansive in its significance. That wider importance is most vivid in the instrumental role Chuco punk played in igniting the Latinx Hardcore punk rock revolution of the 1990s.

Pilsen and Chuco were adjoining constellations in the Latinx hardcore universe. When punx in Pilsen see Martín Sorrondeguy, they yell, "Hey, Martín Crudo!" When punx in Chuco refer to Jenny Cisneros, they clarify it with, "You mean Jenny Sbitch. Right?" The nicknames are simply upshoots of the inextricably intertwined roots of Latinx Hardcore apparent in Sorrondeguy's *Mas Allá de Los Gritos/Beyond the Screams: A U.S. Latino Hardcore Punk Documentary*, where bands like Sbitch and Revolución X are prominently featured.

In 2017, Rafael Uzcátegui, host of the podcast *Imperdibles*, dedicated an entire episode to Revolución X, obsessing over the first album's political importance and how it typifies "a sound that embodies three chords played from Latin America." He imbues the episode with a heightened tone of intrigue as he refers to Revolución X as "una banda fantasma," since nobody supposedly "knows who the band members were."[5]

Chuco punk Gaspar Orozco was Revolución X, though Alex Martínez and Jason Cagann played live with him at times. The podcaster's obsession is not just some hyperbolic expression of gushing fandom. Revolución X, especially their song "I'm Making My Future with the Border Patrol," is foundational to this movement. Scholar Patricia Zavella calls the song "something of an anthem for Latina/o punks."[6] Indeed, when Orozco re-formed the band in 2015 and played the song at a concert in Mexico City, he remembers, "The people knew the lyrics, and they were singing it with me. It was something that we had recorded twenty years earlier!" This scene was even more powerful because most of these punx were Brown.

Ernesto Ybarra is adamant that the sources of this ferocious

Gaspar Orozco, founding member, lead singer, and guitarist of the iconic Revolución X

Chuco punk were "Mexican, Indigenous, and poor kids." Indeed, it was mainly Brown kids who were the architects of this influential punk rock. Journalist Eduardo Cepeda, for instance, described Cedric Bixler-Závala as a "young punk kid who went on to tour the world and knock down doors for future generations of aspiring Latinx post-hardcore kids."[7] Chuco punx were a multiracial, predominantly Brown bunch of misfits who, like their pachuca and pachuco ancestors, were alienated from society and defied conventional modes and mores with a sound and style that changed punk rock for the better.

The vitality and creativity of this scene that was predominantly of color is a profound corrective to the flippant and shallow notion of punk rock as "the first white music since the 1960s psychedelic stuff."[8] Thankfully, there are path breaking works like Francesca T. Royster's writing that challenges supposedly "white genres" like country music, for example. She demonstrates that "rather than asking for a seat at the table, artists . . . are using country music as a way of exploring a more complex Black identity."[9]

Mexican and other Brown kids have similarly nuanced identities to explore that fall outside of the salsa or mariachi or hip-hop that the industry expects to confine us to musically. Punk rock music has always been a medium to explore the intricacy of lives of punx of color, including Chicanx/Latinx lives.

Chuco punk demonstrates that punx of color, and Chicanx/Latinx punx in particular, were not just asking for a seat at the table. They built the damn table, too.

Punx of color have always taken the stage, been in the pit, and shouted and spit from the audience, and the story of Chuco punk demonstrates how these punx of color were always there . . .

As were the women.

"WE WERE THERE."—THE WOMEN OF CHUCO PUNK

> Suggestion: replace the word "fangirl" with "expert" and see what happens.
>
> *Jessica Hopper, music critic and author, quoted in Hannah Ewens's* Fangirls: Scenes from Modern Music Culture

Kate Schellenbach's relentless drumming could be heard in the late 1970s NYC experimental hardcore punk band the Young Aborigines. The gaggle of upstart punx started to embrace the new sound of hip-hop flourishing in the city at the time, and with a new band lineup, they also took on a new name: the Beastie Boys. This new hip-hop sound started working out for Schellenbach and her bandmates when they hired DJ Rick Rubin, who eventually started to collaborate with the new band.

After being out of town for a while, Schellenbach returned to a local NYC haunt, only to run into her bandmates in the Beastie Boys. They were all decked out in matching Puma tracksuits that Rubin had bought the crew.

There wasn't a tracksuit for Schellenbach.

Rubin was frank: "I don't like the way women sound rapping,"[10] and as The Beastie Boys' Adam "Ad Roc" Horovitz, admits, "We kicked Kate [Schellenbach] out of the band because she didn't fit in with this new 'dude thing' we were doing."[11]

Like with raúlsalinas' "La Pachuca" that "remained in their textbooks/ANONYMOUS," Schellenbach, along with hosts of other women, have been literally pushed out, erased, and/or ignored in music and music histories.

They are not anonymous here. Women's perspectives, experiences, and struggles have always been integral to the history of Chuco and Chuco punk. It would have been an effort to leave them out of this story. Who put on the shows? Who wrote the zines? Who sang hardcore punk? By paying attention to the many women, especially Chicanas, and also queer punx involved in the scene, you gain a textured, nuanced, and layered understanding of Chuco punk.

For many, Chuco punk spaces were unique, and punx like Marissa Chávez saw the scene as "the antithesis to machismo culture elsewhere." Lead women in bands, like Jenny Cisneros, for instance, saw that the punk scene attracted people, in particular guys, that were dedicated to values like peace and equality, so her experience was positive and supportive. She explains, "I didn't feel weird about being the only female in the band. I think that I was treated fairly by everybody in the band."

This supportive reality must be held simultaneously with accounts of sexism within the scene. With punx like Bobbie Welch, it was clear that women had played a central role in promoting, but it did not mean that women like punk promoter Jessica Flores did not experience overt and subtle forms of sexism. She explains,

> And it's really hard for girls to be a promoter. I would get people just telling me comments like, 'This is a real good turnout for a girl promoter.' Just stupid shit like that. You know what I mean? And, so Luis [Mota] started getting most of the shows because he's like a dude, ya' know? Maybe it was me, and I didn't want to do it, but it was probably a mixture of a lot of things.

Just like with punx of color, it is imperative to bring women and queer punx into the narrative to counter the knee-jerk tendency among some journalists and punk scholars to ignore them and the range of their experiences in the scene: from the empowering to the dismissive to the dehumanizing.

The moms, gramitas, and queer kids pilgrimaging to the Headstand and the fangirls who music critic Jessica Hopper asks us to see instead as experts were all instrumental players in this creative community.[12]

Challenging conventions in punk rock's DNA and sharing the stories of women and queer punx is in line with that tradition. As Chicana novelist and poet Sandra Cisneros explains, "I'm listening to voices nobody listened to, setting their own lives down how many years later? And that writing is a resistance, an act against forgetting, a war against oblivion against not counting, as women."[13]

This means we have to look beyond breakout bands like ATDI to honor the women and queer punx that were integral to Chuco punk. If not, we're back to "the whole John Lennon and Yoko Ono debacle," according to Lauren Cisneros, where The Beatles were able to prosper from Ono's talent.

Lauren is just as unyielding as Ybarra, when she reminds people, "I always think about how there were girls that were a part of the scene, and it wasn't just about the guys. Like Jenny Cisneros from Sbitch. There were amazing females being a part of that. That's what people need to know. Maybe, it wasn't as all-inclusive as it should have been, but they were there.

"We were there. We were part of it no matter what any guy says or tries to downplay it.

"We were there."

I DON'T WANT TO FORGET

At an El Paso City Council meeting in 2006, the city-backed Glass Beach marketing firm delivered a slide presentation of two contrasting versions of El Paso. The first slide was based on what forty El Pasoans supposedly thought of their city, placed under the PowerPoint heading of "Old Cowboy." To the right was a picture of an anonymous, elderly Mexican man in a white cowboy hat, walking away from ramshackle tiendas. Next to this anonymous man were the words: "Gritty," "Dirty," "Lazy," "Speaks Spanish," "Uneducated."

The subsequent slide provided a stark contrast.

With two glamorous close ups of white Texan actor Matthew McConaughey and Spanish (NOT Mexican) actress Penélope Cruz, the words cascading between the two pictures, under the title of "New West," were "Educated," "Entrepreneurial," "Bilingual," and "Enjoys Entertainment." The presentation caused an uproar over its racist connotations and further galvanized opposition to a development plan that would uproot low-income Mexican residents of the historic Durangito neighborhood of Segundo Barrio.[14] Such views of the city and its people have a deep history. At the end of the nineteenth century, for instance, Anglo-run newspaper editors praised the erasure of Mexican power and culture from El Paso's landscape. For them, "the removal of ancient adobe with all their bad associations means a new life for El Paso."[15]

While centuries apart, the two images of El Paso and its Mexican and Indigenous residents as outmoded, primitive, exotic, and backwards continue to endure in the public consciousness. The city has *never* been a backwater. It has always been a flourishing site of transformative culture. From the rise of *pachuquismo* to ATDI's *Relationship of Command*, Chuco has been the wellspring of cultural innovation and cultural resistance. While creating masterpieces like Don Tosti's "Pachuco Boogie," for instance, a strong sense of pride among communities of color have been at the forefront of the city's innovation and unwillingness to be whitewashed.

This flourishing creativity required destroying limits and borders, which Chuco punx excelled at in the late twentieth and early twenty-first centuries.

They did this by transforming space. With skateboards, they escaped their neighborhoods and explored the city on their own terms. Their shows at places like Oñate's Crossing and the Arboleda House took the power away from bars and clubs and redesigned dry riverbeds and backyards into central live venues. They took ditches and car repair shops to create spaces like the Worm and the Rugburn where punx from throughout the city could congregate. They bent international borders to their will with shows in El Paso and Lencho's Place in

Juárez. Their politics also transcended these borders with the creation of The Mujer Festival. In the rascuache tradition, Chuco punx have always done it themselves, creating and honoring their culture and keeping Chuco alive.

El Paso has also been significant politically, economically, and socially, whether it was under Indigenous, Spanish, Mexican, or American control. Moreover, its relevance nationally and internationally intensified right at the time the second generation of Chuco punk was flourishing. In the late twentieth century, El Paso became ground zero for Silvestre Reyes' radical overhaul of immigration enforcement that was instrumental in fueling a new front in the war on drugs, a transformation that can still be seen along the border today. However, in 2012, the then US congressman Reyes faced a young upstart challenger in his bid for re-election: Beto O'Rourke. The history of Chuco punk came full circle as O'Rourke's focus on bringing an end to the war on drugs helped him beat Reyes, a legendary figure who shaped Juárez/El Paso right when O'Rourke was playing in Foss and putting out records on Western Breed.

O'Rourke's political star also signals to the outside world the importance of this scene and the city's significance, but like with ATDI, the visibility of O'Rourke's political rise belies a centuries-deep history of political rebellion and, even more importantly, of cultural insurgency. Acknowledging the city's significance culturally and politically is all the more urgent in the face of increasing racist violence.

In 2022, the city of now close to 677,456 people was 81.6 percent "Hispanic," and this very feature that makes Chuco special has also made it a target.[16] In August of 2019, a white supremacist from a suburb of Dallas drove to El Paso with one purpose in mind: to "address" what he saw as the "invasion" of "Hispanic" immigrants and the supposed eventual overturn of the political order in Texas. On August 3, he entered a Walmart near the Cielo Vista Mall and murdered twenty-three people.[17]

Once again, the creative community in Chuco responded. Just four days later, the city held a rally with appearances by the likes of Beto O'Rourke and Jim Ward. This feeling of solidarity was not just punk rock in nature, but it permeated the entire creative community, including Grammy nominated singer-songwriter Khalid. In September of 2019, he organized an "El Paso Benefit Concert" and donned an "El Paso Love" sweater as he sang "A Night For Suncity" to El Paso.

Khalid reminded the audience, "The world loves you, El Paso!"[18]

Throughout the city today, you can see school fences in Northeast El Paso filled with colorful plastic cups. When you step far enough away, you can read the rallying cry, "El Paso Strong."

You can also see it in Central El Paso with elegant graffiti adorning cinderblock walls, with the defiant and simple reminder: "United."

It's a powerful feeling of a close-knit community in a large metropolis; it's that timeless feeling of Chuco.

MEMORY AND LEGACY

No longer straining to see El Paso from a swing set in Doña Ana, New Mexico, catching a view of the city is much easier now in my forties.

My favorite way to reach El Paso these days is to leave my family's house in Belén, New Mexico, and drive southeast, away from the raging speed of I-25 into the vast and juniper-filled expanse of the Manzano Mountains and Estancia Valley. There's a feeling along that route, not just the tingling anticipation of seeing El Paso in a few hours, but of something more.

A close friend of mine describes this area as a crossroads of time and space, with the remnants of an ancient lake glimmering before you and major historic sites of both New Mexico's and El Paso's history punctuating this sparse journey. The drive is one that most reminds me of why I love my home, a beloved landscape, my querencia, that is just as much El Paso's as it is New Mexico's.

And while this book has been about history, it is also about sound, and sound resonates. Chuco punk has always been about passionate sound too, inspiring a way of life that still vibrates and transcends space and time.

Gabe González puts it best when he talks about punk in his hometown.

I think the energy and a lot of the bands from that era, even if they were different genres, everyone had the same attack. They all attacked art the same way. It was a desperate need, you know, because we didn't have any outlets.

Such ferocity has not been hidden away in the shelves of youthful rebellion. It continues to endure today.

Punk was not a fad for Marina Monsisvais or her community:

It wasn't a phase. You evolve as you grow. But it's the same ethos, the same viewpoint, the same everything.

Erica Ortegón's life is a testament to how Chuco punk was not a phase even after moving to New Mexico. In 1997, she contributed to her best friend Lindy Hernández's zine *Candy From Strangers*. She was clear in her vision decades ago:

Demand that you live life the way you want it to be. Why should you hold back your desires?[19]

Today, on top of working full-time as a teacher, Ortegón, along with her partner, Ernesto Ybarra, DJ three gigs a week in Albuquerque and each have bands that they play in regularly.

There is no disconnect between the Erica of the nineties and the Erica of 2022. She explains, "I feel because I became part of the punk rock scene, and learned about music, it became the foundation of my life. It carried me for the rest of my life."

For those who were there, the memory of this scene is visceral and enduring, and while punk rock was the focus, connection was at its core. Jason Cagann acknowledges he and his carnalas and carnales created something special, which was "a real kind of spiritual entity of the DIY ethic, a real sense of community that was inspiring."

While power and domination are about division and disconnection, the punx created a Chuco of something more, and as Fill Heimer puts it: "We figured out that we could do it on our own, and we figured out that we needed and loved one another."

Although Chuco punk was a sound and feeling that was unique to El Paso, over time, that sound has reached people all over the world, and it can be intimately accessed any time, straight from your ear buds to the part of you that viscerally connects with sound.

And keeping that fire alive is precisely the point for Martha Yvette Martínez:

> We all have the need to revolutionize things. At one point in our young lives: that fire, that passion that is just written off as teenage angst. I feel like we want to revolutionize things for the better when we're young because of the experiences we live. Some of us continue on that path and really make a positive change in our realm of influence. Most of us suppress that and get lost in adulting and forget that fire, and we just become angry. To me, we all have the ability to change things for the best. All those hopes and changes we want to see. We just have to tap back into that fire that burns in each of us.

According to Martínez, "the fire that burns" is Chuco because, really:

> El Paso is in every one of us.

Acknowledgments

THIS BOOK IS THE RESULT of the profound generosity of a multitude of people, and I will attempt to honor them all here. I want to thank Sheila Rowbotham. She is a tireless and fierce researcher, writer, activist, and mentor. I am indebted to her for indefatigable support and belief in my ability to write. If Sheila created the scaffolding of my academic career and interests, my former colleague, OSU Associate Professor of African American and African Studies Dr. Tiyi Morris shared the critical tools to publish. Thank you for believing in my ability to publish my work when very few did.

I am also thankful for colleagues who brought me into their orbits, so I could catapult into my own: Yolanda Levya, George Lipsitz, Jason Mellard, Oliver Wang, Kevin Eagan, Annette Rodríguez, Mike Tapia, Pamela Radcliff, Sherry Aragón, Charlie Steen, Alex De Vore, Dani Abulhawa, Dawson Barrett, Scott Satterwhite, Alan Parkes, Sarah Downman, and all of my colleagues in the Winona State University Department of Political Science/Public Administration/Ethnic Studies.

The staff and librarians at the University of Texas at El Paso Special Collections and the Darrell Kruger Library at Winona State University fed my voracious appetite for obscure sources to deepen the historical scope of this book, so thank you. I want to also thank Winona State University for generously funding a portion of this research via a 2022 Professional Development Award.

I am deeply indebted to the anonymous peer reviewers who took the time to deepen the research while simultaneously ensuring that my writing was as snappy and engaging as possible. The entire staff at UT Press were also so dynamic, encouraging, and helpful, especially series editor Jessica Hopper, Christina Vargas, Danni Bens, Lynne Ferguson, and Uriel Pérez, and my outstanding copyeditor, Aaron Teel, who patiently scoured my writing to ensure these treasured punx stories could shine in all of their grandeur.

While all these folks are outstanding, the *mero mero* has been UT Press's Casey Kittrell. Casey was more than an editor; he was a coach guiding me through doubts, frustration, and bad drafts. I am deeply appreciative of him hanging in there with me through this process.

Familia is always foundational, and I interpret this broadly; therefore, thank you: *mis padres, mi prima querida* Anita Hartt López, Eric Hamako, Bunny Romero, Helen Peña, Aaron Salinas, *primo talpeño* Vicente Griego, Marisol Encinas, Beata Tsosie-Peña, Luis Peña, Jenn Padilla, Danielle Kellerup, David Perera, Sandra Aguilar, Hugo Cerón, Melissa Ewer, Brenda, Nancy, Jerry Sr., & Jerry Jr. Pacheco, and Luna & Bonita López, my dogs who endured my grumpiness as I struggled with printers, computers, and, more often than not, words. We can go to the dog park, now.

Last, but not least, my deepest appreciation goes to the Chuco punx who not only shared their stories, perspectives, *spantos*, and *mamadas* with me, but were some of the most detailed and generous archivists of flyers and photos that, thus far, have not been archived. Although the oral histories are central to this work, many of the over seventy oral histories, while so valuable, could not fit into this book. Thankfully, with the support of University of Texas at El Paso's Institute for Oral History, especially Drs. Yolanda Leyva and Vianey Závala, many of the stories that could not fit here will inform the work of future researchers. I want to give special shout outs to: Ernesto Ybarra; Erica Ortegón, Mikey Morales, Fill Heimer, Lindy Hernández, Bobbie Welch, David Lucey, Martha Yvette Martínez, Marina Monsisvais, Edmundo Valencia, Gaspar Orozco, Gabe González, Serg Ocadiz, Jason Cagann, Rob Schaffino, and Tony Leal. These are but a few of the people who I pestered with endless texts and phone calls for more and more information, who shared stories, connected me with friends, skated with me in Chuco, and really made me a better person in the process. I would like to name each and every one of these gracious folks, but my editor is going to give me *genio* if I do any more, so I will just say this: Thank you for reminding me that the roots of punk are about love and community, *pues estas palabras que siguen forman una carta de amor, una ballada, un ramo de palabras para celebrar la música y comunidad que nos unen.*

Notes

Oral Histories

David Acosta, Jason Cagann, Marissa Chávez, Jenny Cisneros, Lauren Cisneros, Gabriela Díaz, Jessica Flores, Erik Frescas, Peter Friesen, Gabriel Gónzalez, Fill Heimer, Lindy Hernández, Ed Ivey, David Kirk, Tony Leal, Leah Lloyd, David Lucey, Alex Martínez, Martha Yvette Martínez, Pantaleón Mena, Pancho Mendoza, Sergio "Surge" Mendoza, Marina Monsisvais, Mikey Morales, Luis Mota, Sergio "Serg" Ocadiz, Gaspar Orozco, Sophia Orquiz, Erica Ortegón, Carlos Palacios, Barry Peterson, Kiko Rodríguez, Rob Schaffino, Franko Tormenta, Jacob Trevizo, Edmundo "Mundo" Valencia, Patricia Warren, Barbara "Bobbie" Ann Welch, Ernesto Ybarra, and Jay Youngblood

Preface. Aligning My Coordinates

1. Nick Crossley, *Networks of Sound, Style and Subversion: The Punk and Post-Punk Worlds of Manchester, London, Liverpool and Sheffield, 1975–80* (Manchester, UK: University of Manchester Press, 2015), 3.

2. Gerardo Licón, "Pachucas, Pachucos, and Their Culture: Mexican American Youth Culture of the Southwest, 1910–1955" (PhD dissertation, University of Southern California, 2009), 109, ProQuest Dissertations & Theses Global.

Introduction. "¡Vamonos pa'l Chuco!"

1. Nick Crossley, *Connecting Sounds: The Social Life of Music* (Manchester, UK: University of Manchester Press, 2020), 1–2, 72–83. Although I will be using this more all-embracing understanding of participation in music, I will use the term "music scene," instead of Crossley's "music world," throughout this book since it is the one most commonly used among Chuco punx.

2. Quoted in LeBlanc, *Pretty in Punk: Girls' Gender Resistance in a Boys' Subculture* (New Brunswick, NJ: Rutgers University Press, 2005), 47.

3. Angela McRobbie, *Feminism and Youth Culture: From Jackie to Just Seventeen* (Boston: Unwin Hyman, 1991), xvii.

4. LeBlanc, *Pretty in Punk*, 13.

5. Vivien Goldman, *Revenge of the She-Punks: A Feminist Music History from Poly Styrene to Pussy Riot*, 2nd ed. (Austin, TX: University of Texas Press, 2020), 9.

6. I place "Hispanic" in quotes because, while the US Census Bureau uses this racial/ethnic category to count 62.1 million Americans, many from this community do not use this term. For some, the term's association with Hispania erases the Indigenous, Black, and Asian ancestry of Latinx peoples and their foundational influence on Latinx culture. One helpful source of information on this topic is Laura Gómez's *Inventing Latinos: A New Story of American Racism* (New York: The New Press, 2020) and for a punk challenge to the term listen to former Zeros vocalist and guitarist Robert "El Vez" López's song "Never Been to Spain," where he declares, "Well, I've never been to Spain, so don't call me a Hispanic."

7. United States Census Bureau, "Texas—Race and Hispanic Origin for Selected Large Cities and Other Places: Earliest Census to 1990," accessed November, 27, 2023, https://www2.census.gov/library/working-papers/2005/demo/pop-twps0076/txtab.pdf.

8. United States Census Bureau, "Quick Facts, El Paso city, Texas, El Paso County, Texas," accessed June 25, 2023, https://www.census.gov/quickfacts/fact/table/elpasocitytexas,elpasocountytexas/PST045222.

9. Mykel Board, "Mykel Board Says, 'You're Wrong,'" *Maximum Rocknroll* 34 (March 1986).

10. Quoted in David Pearson, *Rebel Music in the Triumphant Empire: Punk Rock in the 1990s United States* (New York: Oxford University Press, 2021), 133.

11. This is referred to as the "white riot" narrative, a reference to the Clash's 1977 single. Some works in this vein include: Daniel S. Traber, "L.A.'s 'White Minority': Punk and the Contradictions of Self-Marginalization," *Cultural Critique*, no. 48 (Spring 2001), 30–64; Legs McNeil and Gillian McCain, *Please Kill Me: The Uncensored Oral History of Punk* (New York: Grove Press, 1996); and Steven Blush and George Petros, *American Hardcore: A Tribal History* (Port Townsend, WA: Feral House, Inc., 2001).

12. Douglas S. Massey, "Still the Linchpin: Segregation and Stratification in the USA," *Race and Social Problems* 12, no. 1 (March 2020), 8.

13. Michelle Habell-Pallán, *Loca Motion: The Travels of Chicana and Latina Popular Culture* (New York: NYU Press, 2005), 173.

14. Throughout this book, you will see a variety of terms appear to describe the ethnic composition of these punx. The most common term, "Mexican," will be utilized because this is the term most often used among interviewees. However, it is essential to note that this is used as an ethnic designation, not one of citizenship, so when the term is used, it often refers to "Mexican-American" and/or "Chicana/o/x."

15. Sorina Diaconescu, "Secrets of the Sun," *L.A. Weekly*, June 26, 2003, https://www.laweekly.com/secrets-of-the-sun/.

16. Habell-Pallán, *Loca Motion*, 19; Philip Deloria Jr., *Indians in Unexpected Places* (Lawrence, KS: University of Kansas Press, 2004).

17. Monica Perales, *Smeltertown: Making and Remembering a Southwest Border Community* (Chapel Hill: University of North Carolina Press, 2010), 5.

18. Times Staff Report, "El Paso Among 'Top 10 Safest Metro Cities' in the U.S. for 2019," *El Paso Times*, April 24, 2019, https://www.elpasotimes.com/story /news/local/el-paso/2019/04/24/el-paso-ranked-top-10-safest-metro-cities-u-s /3556070002/; "Smart Asset—Safest Cities in America—2023 Edition," Smart Asset, accessed July 3, 2023, https://smartasset.com/data-studies/safest-cities-in -america-2023. In 2019, El Paso was ranked the nation's sixth safest city, and it came in as the twelfth safest city in 2023.

19. Gerardo Licón, "Pachucas, Pachucos, and Their Culture: Mexican American Youth Culture of the Southwest, 1910–1955" (PhD dissertation, University of Southern California, 2009), 119.

20. Quoted in Ricci Chávez Garcia, "Border Hoppin' Hardcore: The Forming of Latina/o Punks' Transborder Civic Imagination on the Bajalta California Borderlands and the Refashioning of Punks' Revolutionary Subjectivity, 1974–79" (master's thesis, California State University, Long Beach, 2014), 81.

21. Ray Hudson, "Regions and Place: Music, Identity, and Place," *Progress in Human Geography* 30, no. 5 (2006): 627.

22. Gloria Anzaldúa, *Borderlands: La Frontera, the New Mestiza*, 4th ed. (San Francisco: Aunt Lute Books, 2007), 25.

23. María Josefina Saldaña-Portillo, *Indian Given: Racial Geographies across Mexico and the United States* (Durham, NC: Duke University Press, 2016), 3.

24. "Issac Brock of Modest Mouse—The Berrics," August 21, 2015, YouTube, https://www.youtube.com/watch?v=fdbzrk6cG7I&t=330s.

25. "Introducing Louder Than a Riot," Louder Than a Riot, June 25, 2023, https://www.npr.org/2020/09/16/913539440/introducing-louder-than-a-riot.

1. "Pachuco Boogie": Culture, Music, and History of Chuco

"Pachuco Boogie" was cited and translated in Paloma Martínez-Cruz, "Un-fixing the Race: Midcentury Sonic Latinidad in the Shadow of Hollywood," *Latino Studies* 14, no. 2 (July 2016): 165–166.

1. Mark Guerrero interview with Edmundo Martínez Tostado, Mark Guerrero Radio (podcast), recorded on July 2, 1998, https://markguerrero.podbean.com /e/don-tosti/.

2. Online Archive of California, "Guide to the Don Tosti Papers CEMA 88, UC Santa Barbara: Biographical/Historical Note," accessed June 26, 2023, https://oac .cdlib.org/findaid/ark: /13030/kt6z09s2g4/entire_text/.

3. Associated Press, "Don Tosti, 81, 'Pachuco' Musician," *New York Times*, August 9, 2004, https://www.nytimes.com/2004/08/09/arts/don-tosti-81-pachuco -musician.html.

4. Luis Alvarez, *The Power of the Zoot: Youth Culture and Resistance during World War II* (Berkeley: University of California Press, 2008), 140.

5. Martínez-Cruz, "Un-fixing the Race," 166.

6. Ann R. Gabbert, "Prostitution and Moral Reform in the Borderlands: El Paso, 1890–1920," *Journal of the History of Sexuality* 12, no. 4 (October 2003): 575.

7. Quoted in Julian Lim, *Porous Borders: Multiracial Migrations and the Law in the U.S.-Mexico Borderlands* (Chapel Hill: The University of North Carolina Press, 2017), 33.

8. Henry Warner Bowden, "Spanish Missions, Cultural Conflict, and the Pueblo Revolt of 1680," *Church History* 44, no. 2 (June 1975): 220.

9. Lim, *Porous Borders*, 34.

10. Jocelyn Bowden, "The Ascarate Grant" (master's thesis, University of Texas at El Paso, August 1952), 60–74, 80–89, ProQuest Dissertations & Theses Global.

11. Ysleta del sur Pueblo, "About Us," accessed June 26, 2023, https://www .ysletadelsurpueblo.org/about-us.

12. Lim, *Porous Borders*, 56.

13. W. H. Timmons, *El Paso: A Borderlands History* (El Paso: Texas Western Press, 1990), 172.

14. David Dorado Romo, *Ringside Seat to a Revolution: An Underground Cultural History of El Paso and Juárez: 1893–1923* (El Paso, TX: Cinco Puntos Press, 2005), 199.

15. Lim, *Porous Borders*, 57.

16. Miguel Juárez, "From Buffalo Soldiers to Redlined Communities: African American Community Building in El Paso's Lincoln Park Neighborhood," *American Studies* 58, no. 3 (2019): 108–109.

17. Juárez, "From Buffalo Soldiers to Redlined Communities," 117.

18. Lim, *Porous Borders*, 49.

19. Romo, *Ringside Seat to a Revolution*, 225–227; Maclovio Perez Jr., "El Paso Bath Riots (1917)," Texas Historical Association website, July 30, 2016, tshaonline .or/handbook/entries/el-paso-bath-house-riots-1917.

20. Gunther Peck, "Free Labor: Immigrant Padrones and Contract Laborers in North America 1885–1925," *Journal of American History* 83, no. 3 (December 1996): 853.

21. Ricci Chávez Garcia, "Border Hoppin' Hardcore: The Forming of Latina/o Punks' Transborder Civic Imagination on the Bajalta California Borderlands and the Refashioning of Punk's Revolutionary Subjectivity, 1974–1999" (master's thesis, California State University, Long Beach, 2014), 18, ProQuest Dissertations & Theses Global. See also, Steven W. Bender, *Greasers and Gringos: Latinos, Law, and the American Imagination* (New York: New York University Press, 2003), xiii.

22. Romo, *Ringside to the Revolution*, 220–221.

23. Shawn Lay, *The Invisible Empire in the West: Toward a New Historical Appraisal of the Ku Klux Klan of the 1920s*, 2nd ed. (Urbana & Chicago: University of Illinois Press, 2004), 70.

24. *El Paso Herald*, June 30, 1921, quoted in Romo, *Ringside to the Revolution*, 140.

25. Lay, *The Invisible Empire in the West*, 81

26. Timmons, *El Paso: A Borderlands History*, 233.

27. Perales, *Smeltertown*, 48–49.

28. Timmons, El Paso: A Borderlands History, 188.

29. Mario T. García, *Desert Immigrants: The Mexicans of El Paso, 1880–1920* (New Haven & London: Yale University Press, 1981), 111–112.

30. Gloria Anzaldúa, *Borderlands; The New Mestiza*, 4th ed. (San Francisco: aunt lute books, 2012), 83.

31. Américo Paredes, *With a Pistol in His Hand: A Border Ballad and Its Hero* (Austin: University of Texas Press, 1958.)

32. Agustin Gurza, "The Mexican Corrido: Ballads of Adversity and Rebellion, Part 3: Two-Part Corridos," The Strachwitz Frontera Collection of Mexican and Mexican American Recordings, https://frontera.library.ucla.edu/blog/2017/11/mexican-corrido-ballads-adversity-and-rebellion-part-3-two-part-corridos.

33. Cited in García, *Desert Immigrants*, 205.

34. María Herrera-Sobek, *Corridos: A Feminist Analysis* (Indianapolis & Bloomington: Indiana University Press, 1993), 72.

35. Elizabeth Salas, *Soldaderas in the Mexican Military: Myth and History* (Austin: University of Texas Press, 1990), 90.

36. Gerardo Licón, "Pachucas, Pachucos, and Their Culture: Mexican American Youth Culture of the Southwest, 1910–1955" (PhD dissertation, University of Southern California, 2009), 109, ProQuest Dissertations & Theses Global. See also Mike Tapia, *Gangs of the El Paso-Juárez Borderland: A History* (Albuquerque: University of New Mexico Press, 2019), 10–16.

37. Catherine S. Ramirez, *The Woman in the Zoot Suit: Gender, Nationalism, and the Cultural Politics of Memory* (Durham & London: Duke University Press, 2009), 55–56.

38. Ramírez, *The Woman in the Zoot Suit*, 25. See also Alejandro Martínez, "Busco Chicas Patas en San Quilmas!" *La Voz de Esperanza*, June 2008, 8.

39. Alvarez, *The Power of the Zoot*, 155–157.

40. Martínez-Cruz, "Un-Fixing the Race," 166.

41. Quoted in Martínez, "Busco Chicas Patas en San Quilmas!," 8.

42. Ricky Moore, "Behind the Song: Marty Robbins, 'El Paso,'" American Songwriter: The Craft of Music, 2019, https://americansongwriter.com/marty-robbins-el-paso/.

43. Timmons, *El Paso: A Borderlands History*, 298.

44. Juárez, "From Buffalo Soldiers to Redlined Communities," 112–115.

45. Conrey Bryson, "Nixon, Lawrence Aaron (1882–1966)," Texas State Historical Association, September 24, 2020, https://www.tshaonline.org/handbook/entries/nixon-lawrence-aaron.

46. Timmons, *El Paso: A Borderlands History*, 251.

47. Timmons, *El Paso: A Borderlands History*, 253.

48. Timmons, *El Paso: A Borderlands History*, 246.

49. Sandra I. Enríquez, " 'A Totality of our Well-Being': The Creation and

Evolution of Centro de Salud Familiar La Fe in South El Paso," in *Civil Rights in Black and Brown: Histories of Resistance and Struggle in Texas*, ed. Max Krochmal and Todd Moye (Austin: University of Texas Press, 2021), 179.

50. Maggie Rivas-Rodríguez, *Texas Mexican Americans and Postwar Civil Rights* (Austin: University of Texas Press, 2015), 47.

51. Howard Campbell and Michael Williams, "Black Barrio on the Border: 'Blaxicans' of Ciudad Juárez," *Journal of Borderlands Studies* 35, no. 1 (2020): 153.

52. "I Fought the Law," Criminal (podcast), April, 9, 2021, https://thisiscriminal. com/episode-162-i-fought-the-law-4-9-2021/.

53. Long John Hunter, "Border Town Blues," *Texas Border Town Blues*, Double Trouble Records, 1986.

54. Associated Press, "Blues Guitarist Long John Hunter Dies at 84," *Billboard*, January 5, 2016, https://www.billboard.com/music/music-news/ long-john-hunter-dies-84-6835249/.

55. "I Fought the Law," Criminal (podcast).

56. John Ratliff, "L.A. Confidential," *Texas Monthly*, May 2000, https://www. texasmonthly.com/articles/l-a-confidential/.

57. Trish Long, "Radio, TV host Steve Crosno Became an El Paso Cultural Icon," *El Paso Times*, August 7, 2020, https://www.elpasotimes.com/story/news/local /el-paso/2020/08/06/radio-tv-host-steve-crosno-became-el-paso-cultural-icon /3288824001/.

58. René Kladzyk, "91 Years of El Paso Music History," *El Paso Matters*, June 12, 2020, https://elpasomatters.org/2020/06/12/91-years-of-el-paso-music-history/.

59. Jasmine Aguilera, "Organizers Remember '71 Chicano Protest at UTEP," *The Prospector*, September 9, 2014, https://www.theprospectordaily.com/2014/09/09/ organizers-remember-71-chicano-protest-at-utep/?print=true.

60. Abelardo Delgado, "Stupid America," in *Chicano: 25 Pieces of a Chicano Mind* (El Paso: Barrio Publications, 1972), 32.

61. Joel Zapata, "Women's Grassroots Vitalization of South El Paso: La Mujer Obrera's Challenge to Gentrification and Neglect," *NACCS Annual Conference Proceedings* 3 (2013), 42–68, San José State University: National Association for Chicana and Chicano Studies, https://scholarworks.sjsu.edu/cgi/viewcontent. cgi?article=1135&context=naccs.

62. *Austin Chronicle*, "Revolution Rock: The Republic Salutes Joe Strummer, Mick Jones, and the Clash's Capital City Clampdown," January 17, 2003, https:// www.austinchronicle.com/music/2003-01-17/122295/#:~:text='%20They%20 were%20really%20fascinated%20with,really%20expect%20anything%20of%20it.

63. Chris Salewicz, *Redemption Song: The Ballad of Joe Strummer, The Definitive Biography* (New York: Farrar, Straus and Giroux, 2008), 222, Kindle.

2. "Electrify Me!" The First Wave of Chuco Punk

The chapter epigraph is from Ricci Chávez Garcia, "Border Hoppin' Hardcore: The Forming of Latina/o Punks' Transborder Civic Imagination on the Bajalta

California Borderlands and the Refashioning of Punk's Revolutionary Subjectivity, 1974–1999" (master's thesis, California State University, Long Beach, 2014), 1–2, ProQuest Dissertations & Theses Global.

1. Leonard Nevarez, "Tito Larriva: the hombre secreto of L.A.'s culture industry," *Musical Urbanism*, January 31, 2012, https://pages.vassar.edu/musicalurbanism /2012/01/31/tito-larriva-the-hombre-secreto-of-l-a-s-culture-industry/.

2. David Reyes and Tom Waldman, *Land of a Thousand Dances: Chicano Rock n' Roll from Southern California* (Albuquerque: University of New Mexico Press, 1998, 2009), 142.

3. Chávez Garcia, "Border Hoppin' Hardcore," 195–196.

4. "Life Is Cheap," *Modern Problems*, Alien Nation, 1981.

5. "Reviews," *Maximum Rocknroll* 1 (July/August 1982).

6. "Singer's Screech Tunes Peculiar Performance," *El Paso Times*, September 21, 1979.

7. "Reviews," *Maximum Rocknroll* 15 (July 1984).

8. *Maxmimum Rocknroll* 25 (May/June 1985)

9. Edna Gundersen, "'Bobbie' Tickets El Paso," *El Paso Times*, January 21, 1983.

10. *El Paso Times*, "A Game Called Promotion," January 25, 1987.

11. *El Paso Times*, "Other Agents Win and Woo New Acts, Too," January 25, 1987.

12. El Paso Times, "A Game Called Promotion," January 25, 1987.

13. Mike Tapia, *Gangs of the El Paso-Juárez Borderlands: A History* (Albuquerque: University of New Mexico Press, 2019), 101.

14. Toby Vail, *Jigsaw* 4 (1991), reprinted in Alison Piepmeier, *Girl Zines (Making Media, Doing Feminism* (New York: New York University Press, 2009), 1.

15. Adam Wilson, *Safety in Numbers: My Journey with L.A. Punk Rock Gangs, 1982–1992* (self-published, 2016), 19–20.

16. "Schaffino," *Acrobatic Tenement*, Flipside Records, 1997.

17. "Uglor@3Fountains 1988 El Paso, TX!," YouTube, accessed June 28, 2023, https://m.youtube.com/watch?v=YSbXK8Qoyq0.

18. "Episode 185—Cedric Bixler-Zavala (At the Drive-In, The Mars Volta, Foss, Antemasque, Anywhere, De Facto etc . . .)" Turned out a Punk podcast, September 18, 2018, https://podcasts.apple. com/us/podcast/footnote-185-cedric-bixler-zavala-at-drive-in-mars/ id940288964?i=1000420340549.

19. Ensminger, *Visual Vitriol*, 107.

20. Iain Borden, "Movement without Words: An Intersection of Lefebvre and the Urban Practice of Skateboarding," in *The Routledge Handbook of Henri Lefebvre, The City and Urban Society*, ed. Michael E. Leary-Owhin and John P. McCarthy (Milton Park: Routledge, 2020).

21. Dani Abulhawa, *Skateboarding and Femininity: Gender, Space-Making, and Expressive Movement* (Milton Park, UK: Routledge, 2020), 37.

22. Jim Ward Interview—"Life Is to Live," April 21, 2018, YouTube, https:// www.youtube.com/watch?v=jt5HjLyqqjk&t=77s.

23. See Michael Kimmel Guyland: *The Perilous World Where Boys Become Men, Understanding the Critical Years Between 16 and 26* (New York: HarperCollins, 2018) and Niobe Way, *Deep Secrets: Boys' Friendships and the Crisis of Connection* (Boston, MA: Harvard University Press, 2011).

24. Abulhawa, *Skateboarding and Femininity*, 19.

25. Abulhawa, *Skateboarding and Femininity*, 28.

26. Nancy Hamilton, "Ysleta, TX," February 1, 1996, Texas State Historical Association website, https://www.tshaonline.org/handbook/entries/ysleta-tx.

27. Yolanda Leyva, unpublished manuscript, "Cotton's Paradise: Coerced Labor and the Right to Live during the Great Depression in El Paso," May 5, 2022.

28. Meena Thiruvengadam, "Apparel Industry No Longer a Good Fit in El Paso," Institute for Agriculture & Trade Policy website, October 15, 2005, https://www.iatp.org/news/apparel-industry-no-longer-a-good-fit-in-el-paso; Joel Zapata, "La Mujer Obrera of El Paso," Texas Historical Association, November 22, 2013, https://www.tshaonline.org/handbook/entries/la-mujer-obrera-of-el-paso; B. Medalille and A. Wheat, "Faded Denim: NAFTA Blues," *Multinational Monitor* 18, no. 12 (1997): 23–26.

29. Mykel Board, "Mykel Board Says, 'You're Wrong,'" *Maximum Rocknroll* 34 (March 1986).

30. Devon Morph, "Interview with Not So Happy," *Maximum Rocknroll* 125 (October 1993). Box 3, Folder 13 MAXIMUM ROCKNROLL, no. 125 1993 October, Special Collections at Claremont Colleges.

31. *Book Your Own Fuckin' Life* 2 (1993). Known as the "most important resource of the underground punk scene," *Book Your Own Fuckin' Life* was the result of a collaboration between Berkeley-based MaximumRockNRoll and Minneapolis-based Profane Existence. Its extensive listing of bands, distributors, and venues, organized by country and state, empowered punk bands to tour without tons of money or a booking agent.

32. *Book Your Own Fuckin' Life* 2 (1993).

33. Angela McRobbie, *Feminism and Youth Culture: From Jackie to Seventeen* (Boston: Unwin Hyman, 1991), xvii.

34. "Household Income in Northwest, El Paso, Texas," Statistical Atlas, accessed June 28, 2023, https://statisticalatlas.com/neighborhood/Texas/El-Paso/Northwest/Household-Income.

35. "Household Income in Lower Valley, El Paso, Texas, Statistical Atlas, accessed June 28, 2023, https://statisticalatlas.com/neighborhood/Texas/El-Paso/Lower-Valley/Race-and-Ethnicity.

36. Lauren Villagran, "Before Flint, Before East Chicago, There was Smeltertown," NRDC, November 29, 2016, https://www.nrdc.org/stories/flint-east-chicago-there-was-smeltertown.

37. Marc-Stefan Andres, "Omar Rodríguez-López: No Life without Pain," Chart, Notes to Consider, accessed June 28, 2023, https://chart.cloudshill.com/omar-rodriguez-lopez-no-life-without-pain/.

38. "Startled Calf – Live @ Coronado High School 12/14/91," YouTube, accessed September 19, 2023, https://www.youtube.com/watch?v=31lxoKgobM8.

39. David Dorado Romo, *Ringside Seat to a Revolution: An Underground Cultural History of El Paso and Juárez: 1893–1923* (El Paso, TX: Cinco Puntos Press, 2005), 179–181.

40. "Binational Population Data in Sister Cities along the Rio Grande," Texas Commission on Environmental Quality, accessed June 28, 2023, https://www.tceq.texas.gov/border/population.html.

41. Quoted in Timothy J. Dunn, *Blockading the Border and Human Rights: The El Paso Operation That Remade Immigration Enforcement* (Austin: University of Texas Press, 2009), 22.

42. Dunn, *Blockading the Border and Human Rights*, 26, 37–50.

3. "Rascuache": The "Second Generation" Finds Its Sound

1. *Candy From Strangers* zine, Issue #3. From the personal collection of Lindy Hernández.

2. Habell-Pallan, *Loca Motion*, 150.

3. While I use the term "chingona" to mean "badass woman," I also embrace the term in a way that also embraces all genders. The following work by Alma Zaragoza-Petty is especially informative in the use of this term: *Chingona: Owning Your Inner Badass for Healing and Justice* (Minneapolis, MN: Broadleaf Books, 2022).

4. *Book Your Own Fuckin' Life 4* (1995).

5. *Book Your Own Fucking Life 3* (1994).

6. *Book Your Own Fuckin' Life 4* (1995).

7. *Book Your Own Fuckin' Life 5* (1996).

8. *Book Your Own Fuckin' Life 4* (1995).

9. *Book Your Own Fuckin' Life 4* (1995).

10. Denise Nelson, "Jim Ward: Guided by Music," *Fusion Magazine*, October 20, 2016, accessed November 25, 2020, https://thefusionmag.com/jim-ward/.

11. David Pearson, *Rebel Music in the Triumphant Empire: Punk Rock in the 1990s United States* (New York: Oxford University Press, 2021), 59–60.

12. Zapata, "La Mujer Obrera of El Paso."

13. "Faded Denim: NAFTA Blues," 23–26.

14. Kathleen Staudt, *Violence and Activism at the Border: Gender, Fear, and Everyday Life in Ciudad Juárez* (Austin: University of Texas Press, 2008), 81.

15. Petra Leaders for Justice, "Cecilia Rodriguez, 100 Heroes, 25 Years," accessed June 30, 2023, http://petrafoundation.org/fellows/cecilia-rodriguez/index.html.

16. George A. Collier with Elizabeth Lowery Quaratiello, *Basta! Land & The Zapatista Rebellion in Chiapas*, revised ed. (Oakland, CA: Food First Books, 1999), 87–90.

17. Quoted in Ricci Chávez Garcia, "Border Hoppin' Hardcore: The Forming of Latina/o Punks' Transborder Civic Imagination on the Bajalta California

Borderlands and the Refashioning of Punk's Revolutionary Subjectivity, 1974–1999" (master's thesis, California State University, Long Beach, 2014), 192, ProQuest Dissertations & Theses Global.

18. Revolución X, *E.Z.L.N.*, New Wave Records, Toxic Grafity Records, !Angrr!, Ineptie, 1994.

19. Revolución X, "I'm Making My Future with the Border Patrol," *E.Z.L.N.*, New Wave Records, Toxic Grafity Records, !Angrr!, Ineptie, 1994. Lyrics reprinted with permission from Gaspar Orozco.

20. Patricia Zavella, "Beyond the Screams: Latino Punkeros Contest Nativist Discourses," *Latin American Perspectives* 39, no. 2 (March 2012): 37.

21. Timothy J. Dunn, *Blockading the Border and Human Rights: The El Paso Operation That Remade Immigration Enforcement* (Austin: University of Texas Press, 2009), 1–4, 52–60.

22. Sbitch, "Pure Death," *Sbitch/P.U.S.-Split*, Revolt Tapes and You're Not Normal Records, 1998. Lyrics used with permission of Jenny Cisneros.

23. *Beyond the Screams/ Más Allá de Los Gritos: A U.S. Latino Hardcore Punk Documentary*, directed by Martín Sorrondeguy (1999), YouTube, https://www.youtube.com/watch?v=iYph2q44MQU&t=124s.

24. Susan Grossman et al., "Pilsen and The Resurrection Project: Community Organization in a Latino Community," *Journal of Poverty* 4, no. 1/2 (2000), 133. Pew Research Center, "Hispanic Population and Dispersion across U.S. Counties, 1980–2020," February 3, 2022, https://www.pewresearch.org/hispanic/interactives/hispanic-population-by-county/.

25. Zavella, "Beyond the Screams," 37.

26. Habell-Pallan, *Loca Motion*, 157.

27. *Candy From Strangers* zine, Issue #3.

28. Joel, "Abolish the White Punk," *Profane Existence* 37 (1998). Habell-Pallan, *Loca Motion*, 150.

29. Habell-Pallan, *Loca Motion*, 150.

30. Unrecorded track. Translation and reproduction with permission from Gaspar Orozco.

31. *Book Your Own Fuckin' Life* 4 (1995).

32. *Book Your Own Fuckin' Life* 5 (1996).

33. Fixed Idea, "Chucotown Ska," Oofas Records, August 1996. Permission to reproduce lyrics to "Chucotown Ska" given by Fill Heimer to author, April 21, 2020.

34. Dan Ozzi, *Sellout: The Major-Label Feeding Frenzy That Swept Punk, Emo, and Hardcore, 1994–2007* (Boston/New York: Mariner Books, 2021), 134; Jim Ward Interview—Life Is to Life, (2017), YouTube, accessed June 30, 2023, https://www.youtube.com/watch?v=jt5HjLyqqjk.

35. Lindy Hernández, Issue #1, *Candy From Strangers*, from the personal collection of Lindy Hernández.

36. *Anti-Ignorance Zine* #1, "Our Cause," from the personal collection of Erica Ortegón.

37. "Rugburn Announcement," from the personal collection of Erica Ortegón.

38. "La Escena de Rock de Los 90s," *Fusion Magazine*, November 30, 2016. Translation by Edmundo Valencia. https://thefusionmag.com/la-escena-de-rock -de-los-90s-en-juarez/.

39. *Book Your Own Fuckin' Life* 5 (1996).

40. "Episode 185—Cedric Bixler-Závala (At the Drive-In, The Mars Volta, Foss, Antemasque, Anywhere, De Facto etc . . .)," Turned out a Punk (podcast), September 18, 2018, https://podcasts.apple.com/us/podcast/footnote-185-cedric -Bixler-Závala-at-drive-in-mars/id940288964?i=1000420340549.

41. María Josefina Saldaña-Portillo, *Indian Given: Racial Geographies across Mexico and the United States* (Durham, NC: Duke University Press, 2016), 3.

42. Dani Abulhawa, "Female Skateboarding: Re-writing Gender," *A Postgraduate eJournal of Theater and Performing Arts* 3, no. 1 (Spring 2008): 57–59.

43. Hanif Abdurraqib, "I Wasn't Brought Here, I Was Born: Surviving Punk Rock Long Enough to Find Afro Punk," in *They Can't Kill Us Till They Kill Us* (Columbus, OH: Two Dollar Radio, 2017), 54–55.

44. Rope, "Leave Me Alone," *Fall on Deaf Ears and Rope: In Memory, 1979– 1997*, Western Breed Records, 1997.

45. Leah Lloyd, Sara Reiser, and Laura Beard, *Femme Fatale*, May 1996/June 1996, from the personal collection of Deana Montoya.

46. Lloyd, Reiser, and Beard, *Femme Fatale*.

47. Booklet: "In Memory, Sara Reiser, Laura Beard (1979–1997)," in *Fall on Deaf Ears and Rope: In Memory, 1979–1997*, Western Breed Records, 1997.

48. *Candy From Strangers*, Vol. 1, from the personal collection of Lindy Hernández.

49. *Candy From Strangers*, Vol. 2, from the personal collection of Lindy Hernández.

50. Jenny Cisneros, *Puro Queso Zine* #1, from the personal collection of Lindy Hernández.

51. Alison Piepmeir, *Girl Zines: Making Media, Doing Feminism* (New York: New York University Press, 2009), 2–4.

52. "Nah, nah, nah, . . . It's Going to Be Cool: Jim Ward at TedXEl Paso," December 5, 2013, YouTube, https://www.youtube.com/watch?v=YAaD-3lnmI4.

53. Ozzi, *Sellout*, 135–136.

54. Lloyd, Reiser, and Beard, *Femme Fatale*.

55. "Leap onto I-10 Kills 23-Year-Old," *El Paso Herald Post*, February 16, 1996.

56. At the Drive-In, *Acrobatic Tenement*, Fearless Records, 1996.

57. Sbitch, "Satisfy the Instinct." Lyrics used with permission from Jenny Cisneros.

58. Sandra Cisneros, "¡Que Vivan Los Colores!," *A House of My Own: Stories from My Life*, 173.

4. "This Is Forever": Indelible Chuco

The first chapter epigraph is from Leah Lloyd, Sara Reiser, and Laura Beard, *Femme Fatale*, May 1996/June 1996, from the personal collection of Deana Montoya.

1. Rachel Romero, "Two UT El Paso Students Die in Car Accident," University of Texas at El Paso, *The Prospector*, March 25, 1997. See also Rachel Romero, "Two Teens, One Man Die in Separate Accidents," El Paso Herald-Post, March 24, 1997.

2. Lloyd, Reiser, and Beard, *Femme Fatale*.

3. Alex Durán, "The Man That Is the Headstand," *Fusion Magazine*, October 19, 2012.

4. *Book Your Own Fuckin' Life* 6 (1997).

5. *Book Your Own Fuckin' Life* 9 (2001).

6. David Pearson, *Rebel Music in the Triumphant Empire: Punk Rock in the 1990s United States* (New York: Oxford University Press, 2021), 219.

7. *Book Your Own Fuckin' Life* 6 (1997).

8. Pearson, *Rebel Music in the Triumphant Empire*, 9.

9. Jessica Hopper, "Emo: Where the Girls Aren't," in *The First Collection of Criticism by a Living Female Rock Critic* (Chicago: featherproof books, 2015), 15.

10. *Book Your Own Fuckin' Life* 9 (2001).

11. "Interpunk: SIVA," accessed July 2, 2023, https://www.interpunk.com/band.cfm?BandID=4656&.

12. *Book Your Own Fuckin' Life* 6 (1997).

13. Peter J. D'Angelo, "Behind the Curtain: Egon," *All Music*, accessed July 2, 2023, https://www.allmusic.com/album/behind-the-curtain-mw0001277034.

14. *Book Your Own Fucking Life* 4 (1995).

15. "Sbitch: Interview by Michael Thorn," *Maximum Rocknroll* 219 (2001).

16. Dan Ozzi, *Sellout! The Major-Label Feeding Frenzy That Swept Punk, Emo, and Hardcore, 1994-2007* (Boston/New York: Mariner Books, 2021), 138–143.

17. Ozzi, *Sellout*, 152–153.

18. *Book Your Own Fuckin' Life* 4 (1995).

19. "Top 20 Albums of the Year," *Spin*, January 2001, 73.

20. "Abolish White Punk," *Profane Existence* 37 (1998), 28–29.

21. Ozzi, *Sellout*, 159.

22. Ozzi, *Sellout*, 147.

23. Neil Strauss, "At the Drive-In's Identity Crisis," *Rolling Stone*, February 15, 2001, https://www.rollingstone.com/music/music-news/at-the-drive-ins-identity-crisis-242873/.

24. Lanre Bakare, "Interview: 'It Was Cool to Be Misogynist': At the Drive-In on Fights, Drugs, and the Dark Days of Nu-Metal," *The Guardian*, November 9, 2017, https://www.theguardian.com/music/2017/nov/09/it-was-cool-to-be-misogynist-at-the-drive-in-on-fights-drugs-and-the-dark-days-of-nu-metal. See also Ozzi, *Sellout*, 158-162.

25. The insights about ATDI containing divergent sonic trajectories was informed by Hanif Abdurraqib's "Cut Away, Cut Away: At the Drive In's Lifetime of Stops and Starts," NPR, May 4, 2017, https://www.npr.org/sections/therecord /2017/05/04/526823806/cut-away-cut-away-at-the-drive-ins-lifetime-of-stops -and-starts.

26. Peter Andreas, *Border Games: Policing the U.S.-Mexico Divide* (Ithaca & London: Cornell University Press, 2000), xvii.

27. Peter Andreas, "Redrawing the Line: Borders and Security at the Twenty-First Century," *International Security* 28, no. 2 (Fall 2003): 87–89.

28. Timothy Dunn, *Blockading the Border and Human Rights: The El Paso Operation That Remade Immigration Enforcement* (Austin: University of Texas Press, 2009), 166.

29. Manny Fernandez, "U.S. Troops Went to the Border in 1997. They Killed an American Boy," *New York Times*, November 27, 2018, https://www.nytimes. com/2018/11/27/us/esequiel-hernandez-death-border-mexico.html.

30. Lindy Hernández, *Candy From Strangers* # 3, from the personal collection of Lindy Hernández.

31. Teresa Rodriguez, Diana Montane with Lisa Politzer, *The Daughters of Juarez: A True Story of the Serial Murder South of the Border* (New York: Atria Books, 2007), 92–93.

32. Kathleen Staudt, *Violence and Activism at the Border: Gender, Fear, and Everyday Life in Ciudad Juárez* (Austin: University of Texas Press, 2008), 10.

33. See also Alicia Schmidt Camacho, "Ciudadana X: Gender Violence and the Denationalization of Women's Rights in Ciudad Juárez," *The New Centennial Review* 5, no. 1 (Spring 2005): 255–292; Alicia Gaspar de Alba, "The Maquiladora Murders, or, Who is Killing the Women of Juárez, Mexico? *Latino Policy & Issues Brief,* no. 7, August 2003.

34. Diana Washington Valdez, *The Killing Fields: Harvest of Women, The Truth about Mexico's Bloody Border Legacy* (Burbank, CA: Peace at the Border Publishers, 2006), 2.

35. Quoted in Judith Matloff, "Six Women Murdered Each Day as Femicide in Mexico Nears a Pandemic," *Al Jazeera America*, January 4, 2015, http://america. aljazeera.com/multimedia/2015/1/mexico-s-pandemicfemicides.html.

36. Staudt, *Violence and Activism at the Border*, 2.

37. Schmidt Camacho, "Ciudadana X," 259.

38. Rodríguez et al., *The Daughters of Juárez*, 102–103.

39. Staudt, *Violence and Activism at the Border*, 82; New Mexico State University, "Esther Chavez Cano, 1933-2009, Biography," accessed December 5, 2023, https://libexhibits.nmsu.edu/onlinexhibits/chavez-cano/index.html..

40. *Spotlight Initiative*, "Casa Amiga: A Safe Space in One of Mexico's Most Dangerous Cities for Women," June 20, 2022, https://www.spotlightinitiative.org/ news/casa-amiga-safe-space-one-mexicos-most-dangerous-cities-women.

41. Stuadt, *Violence and Activism at the Border*, 81–82.

42. At The Drive-In, "Invalid Litter Dept.," *Relationship of Command*, Grand Royale, 2000.

43. J. Anthony Monarez, "Rock 'n' Roll Professor," *Prospector*, August 26, 2008.

44. At the Drive-In, "Invalid Litter Dept.," directed by Anton Corbijn, 2001, https://www.youtube.com/watch?v=8wR1MVdDmUA&list=RD8wR1MVdDmUA&start_radio=1.

45. Laura Cruz, "2000 Fight Violence to Women at Festival," *El Paso Times*, July 15, 2002.

46. Michael D. Hernandez, "Festival to Raise Awareness of Crimes against Juárez Women," *El Paso Times*, Friday, July 5, 2002.

47. Quoted in Ozzi, *Sellout*, 140–141.

48. Julia Monárrez Fragoso, " Feminicidio sexual serial en Ciudad Juárez: 1993-2001," *Debate Feminista* 25 (April 2002), 299. (Translation of passage by author.)

49. At the Drive-In, "One Armed Scissor," *Relationship of Command*, Grand Royale, 2000.

Conclusion. "El Paso Is in Every One of Us!"

1. "The Chats Live in El Paso, TX: Sicteens cover," May 22, 2022, Lowbrow Palace, El Paso, TX, YouTube, https://www.youtube.com/watch?v=kjCgEjGhGxk.

2. *El Paso Punk Zine*, from the personal collection of Fill Heimer.

3. "Latinopia Word Raul Salinas Hail Pachuco," 1973, Vimeo, accessed July 3, 2023, https://vimeo.com/203508260.

4. Hanif Abdurraqib's "Cut Away, Cut Away: At the Drive In's Lifetime of Stops and Starts," NPR, May 4, 2017, https://www.npr.org/sections/therecord/2017/05/04/526823806/cut-away-cut-away-at-the-drive-ins-lifetime-of-stops-and-starts.

5. "Revolucion X en Imperdibles," March 27, 2017, https://noesfm.com/revolucion-x-en-imperdibles/.

6. Patricia Zavella, "Beyond the Screams: Latino Punkeros Contest Nativist Discourses," *Latin American Perspectives* 39, no. 2 (2012): 37.

7. Eduardo Cepeda, "What It Was Like to Be in a Punk Band with Beto O'Rouke According to Cedric Bixler Zavala," *Remezcla*, August 31, 2018, https://remezcla.com/features/music/beto-orourke-punk-band-foss-cedric-bixler-zavala/.

8. Mykel Board, "Mykel Board Says, 'You're Wrong,'" *Maximum Rocknroll 34* (March 1986).

9. Francesca Royster, *Black Country Music: Listening for Revolutions* (Austin: University of Texas Press, 2022), 175.

10. Jessica Grose, "The Long Lost Beastie Girl," *Slate*, April 26, 2011, https://slate.com/human-interest/2011/04/the-long-lost-beastie-girl.html.

11. "Beastie Boys on Forcing Drummer Kate Schellenbach Out—and Why They Regret It," *PBS News Hour*, May 24, 2019, YouTube, https://www.youtube.com/watch?v=mheuvbNooek.

12. Hannah Ewens, *Fangirls: Scenes from Modern Music Culture* (Austin: University of Texas Press, 2020), ii.

13. Sandra Cisneros, "I Can Live *Sola* and I Love to Work," in *A House of My Own: Stories from My Life* (New York: Vintage, 2015), 140.

14. Christopher Hooks, "Beto Versus the Barrio," *The American Prospect*, March 15, 2019, https://prospect.org/civil-rights/beto-versus-barrio/. See also "Beto O'Rourke's Political Career Drew on Donations from the Pro-GOP Business Establishment," *Texas Tribune*, March 15, 2019, https://www.texastribune.org/2019/03/15/beto-orourke-drew-donations-pro-gop-political-establishment/, and Martin Paredes, "Glass Beach: The Story Behind the Glass Beach Study," *El Paso News*, July 29, 2020, https://elpasonews.org/2020/07/29/the-story-behind-the-glass-beach-study/.

15. Quoted in Monica Perales, *Smeltertown: Making and Remembering a Southwest Border Community* (Chapel Hill: University of North Carolina Press, 2010), 46.

16. US Census Bureau, "Quick Facts: El Paso city, Texas; El Paso County, Texas," accessed October 2, 2023, https://www.census.gov/quickfacts/fact/table/elpasocitytexas,elpasocountytexas/PST045222.

17. The victims were Jordan Anchondo, Andre Anchondo, Arturo Benavidez, Javier Rodriguez, Sara Eshter Regalado Moriel, Adolfo Cerros Hernandez, Gloria Irma Marquez, Maria Eugenia Legarreta Rothe, Ivan Manzano, Juan de Dios Velazquez Chairez, David Johnson, Leonardo Campos Jr., Maribel Campos (Loya), Angelina Silva Englisbee, Maria Flores, Raul Flores, Jorge Calvillo Garcia, Alexander Gerhard Hoffman, Luis Alfonso Juarez, Elsa Mendoza de la Mora, Margie Reckard, Teresa Sanchez, and Guillermo "Memo" Garcia.

18. "Khalid Hosts El Paso Benefit Concert," September 3, 2019, YouTube, https://www.youtube.com/watch?v=YL8bSzPJhY0.

19. *Candy From Strangers* #3, from the personal collection of Lindy Hernández.

Photo Credits

Index